Dec. 6th 1974.

..... in case of a departmental move across the water!

Have another successful, healthy year.

Love,

Mimi and Stephen.

ON IRELAND

CECIL KING

ON IRELAND

Jonathan Cape Thirty Bedford Square London

First published 1973
© 1973 by Cecil King

Jonathan Cape Ltd, 30 Bedford Square, London W C 1

I S B N 0 224 00956 7

The author and publisher are grateful to
Hamish Hamilton Ltd for permission to quote
certain passages from *The Great Hunger,* by
Cecil Woodham-Smith, © 1962 by Cecil
Woodham-Smith, and to Thames and Hudson Ltd
for permission to quote from *A Concise History of
Ireland,* by Maire and Conor Cruise O'Brien

Printed in Great Britain
by Compton Press, Salisbury
bound by G. & J. Kitcat Ltd, London

CONTENTS

ACKNOWLEDGMENTS

For the historical narrative I have been entirely dependent on the work of historians of Ireland. I have found helpful *A New History of Ireland,* by R. Dudley Edwards, *A Concise History of Ireland,* by Maire and Conor Cruise O'Brien, *Belfast: Approach to Crisis – A Study of Belfast Politics, 1613–1970,* by Ian Budge and Cornelius O'Leary, *Tudor and Stuart Ireland* by Margaret MacCurtain, *Ireland Before the Famine 1798–1848,* by Gearoid O'Tuathaigh, and *Ulster* by the Sunday Times Insight Team.

While recognizing the great assistance I have had from these authors and their books I would like to thank particularly warmly Dr James Lydon for *The Lordship of Ireland in the Middle Ages.* It was as a result of reading this book that I was moved to write my own. Another author on whom I was particularly dependent was Professor F. S. L. Lyons, whose *Ireland since the Famine* is an excellent account of events up to 1969. And finally I must pay my warmest tribute to Mrs Cecil Woodham-Smith for her book *The Great Hunger* – a history classic if ever there was one.

For historical facts I have picked the brains of others. The opinions are my own.

INTRODUCTION

This book is not a work of scholarship or research: it is an attempt by an Irishman to explain to Englishmen why the Irish are as they are. It is not an apology but an attempt to show that just because the two peoples live in adjacent islands they are not the same: they are different peoples still further differentiated by a different history.

I was born in London, but between the ages of four and nineteen my home was in Dundrum, on the south side of Dublin. I was mostly educated in England, at Winchester College and Christ Church, Oxford, but spent some eighteen months at a day school in St Stephen's Green. My father was born of Irish parents in Madras and was brought up in the west of Ireland, in County Clare. My mother was born at Chapelizod, a village on the north side of Dublin. My father, my grandfather and my great-grandfather were all graduates of Trinity College, Dublin. When my father retired from the Indian Civil Service he became Professor of Oriental Languages at his old university. He learnt Irish and in time became one of the selectors for the Professorship of Irish at T.C.D. My mother's father was English, but her mother was Scots Irish. My remoter ancestors were Dublin Protestants – schoolmasters, doctors, booksellers, silversmiths and brewers. My great-great-grandfather, who was a bookseller and publisher in Westmoreland Street, Dublin, lost his business, which largely depended on official favour, when it was found he was dabbling in the nationalist politics of the early years of the last century. My grandfather, a doctor in the Indian Medical Service, was a Fenian, and surprised to find that he did not receive the promotion to which he felt his medical service entitled him. His brother, my grand-uncle and godfather, was the author of books on Swift and Goldsmith, and was for many years President of the Irish Literary Society in London.

My introduction to Irish politics was as a child in the early years of the century when walking beside the pram of my younger brother and sister. We often used to see our favourite roadman drilling in a field beside the road. Later, as a schoolboy, in the Easter Rising of 1916, I stood on the roof of a convent near my home and saw the naval shells from H.M.S. *Helga* bursting over the area round O'Connell Street. I was afterwards driven round to see the damage. The clearest memory I have of those days is watching the Sherwood Foresters marching into Dublin along the Stillorgan Road from Kingstown. It was these troops that were ambushed at the Mount Street Bridge, where many were killed.

I give these facts as my claim to speak about Ireland and Irish affairs. My motives are a great love of Ireland and a desire to see her people living at peace.

Chapter one

IRELAND BEFORE A.D. 800

At the period of history for which we have the earliest
written records Ireland was populated by Celts, but
not of the same branch as the Welsh. When they came
to Ireland is not known, but it does appear from early
megalithic monuments that there were earlier inhabitants of Ireland. In the West there are some very dark
people, and it used to be said that their ancestors were
Spanish sailors wrecked in the flight of the Armada
in 1588, although it is more likely that they were
descendants of pre-Celtic immigrants, perhaps related
to the Basques. The Celts in Ireland were an artistic
people and their gold work of the Bronze Age is as
fine as any in Europe, and is found scattered all over
the West.

The first hard fact about early Irish history is a
negative one – Ireland was never occupied by the
Romans. I am not qualified to give an assessment of
the influence of Rome on English society, but one only
has to notice the place names to realize its extent,
even today. Not only did they found such cities as
Winchester, Colchester, Gloucester and Worcester,
but also London and York and a number of Welsh
places with names beginning with Caer-. (This was a
corruption of *castrum,* a military camp, which in
England took the form '-chester' or '-cester'.) Not only
did the Romans found these towns, they developed a

network of excellent roads which formed the basis of our road system until this century. Their influence did not extend beyond Hadrian's Wall near the Scottish border and was far more pervasive in the south than in the north and west.

In addition to towns and roads the Romans installed a system of central government, a legal code, coinage and close relations with the continent of Europe. Roman rule continued for some 350 years, and though it was succeeded by some centuries of disorder, the influence of Rome was too powerful ever to have been eliminated.

In Ireland this whole experience was omitted. Roman contacts with Ireland seem to have been minimal – limited to a little trade evidenced by a few coin hoards and little else. The principal introduction from England was Christianity, which was brought by missionaries at the very end of the period of Roman rule in England. The provision of good roads, of a strong central government such as England enjoyed under the Romans, was not brought to Ireland for more than 1000 years.

The Romans left England in A.D. 410, and it was in 431 that the first missionary, one Palladius, was sent by Pope Celestine to Ireland. We know nothing more of Palladius, but it was in the succeeding decades that Christianity really took root in Ireland. No doubt other missionaries were involved, but the most famous was St Patrick, who made Armagh his ecclesiastical capital, as it still is for both the Catholic and the Anglican Churches. St Patrick seems to have been an Englishman who was carried off to Ireland in a raid, escaped, but came back to Ireland to preach the

Gospel. In a dream he saw a letter inscribed 'the voice of the Irish', and as he read he heard the voices of people near the Western Sea, who cried out, 'We pray thee, holy youth, to come and again walk among us.'

A particularly glorious period of Irish history followed the emergence of Christianity. Previously there had been no written language, though Ogham script served for gravestones. Writing had been thought destructive of concentration and of memory, as indeed it is. But once writing was accepted, the Irish scholars of the sixth and succeeding centuries made splendid use of their opportunities. It has been claimed that it was during this period that Ireland became a major cultural centre for the whole of Europe. The Irish manuscripts of the sixth and seventh centuries are magnificently illustrated and in spite of long periods of neglect have survived remarkably well. One of the finest, the book of Durrow, was at one time kept by a man who used it to cure sick cattle by dipping it in water which they were made to drink! One of these manuscripts is believed to be by the hand of St Columba, the great Irish missionary, and to be the oldest manuscript in western Europe. St Columba's name in Irish is Columbcille – the Dove of the Church. He was a member of the great family of O'Neill that has played a prominent part in the history of Ireland for the last 1400 years. There is no family in Europe with a longer family tree.

St Columba was an heir to the kingship of Tara and a member of the literary class. His family connections added prestige to his missionary efforts, which led to the founding of the monasteries of Iona, in

13

Argyllshire, and Lindisfarne, in Northumberland. Northumbria in turn became one of the cultural centres of Europe before the area was devastated by William the Conqueror, a disaster from which it never really recovered.

The Book of Kells was the final achievement of this magnificent creative period. For its early date this is the finest European manuscript in existence and indeed is not to be outshone by any manuscript of any date.

The flowering of Christianity not only led to the production of superb manuscripts. It also produced work in metal of the very highest quality. The Ardagh Chalice of silver, decorated with gold filigree enamel and gilt bronze, is of the finest quality, judged by any standard of time and place.

Ecclesiastical architecture was not so remarkable, but we are dealing with the period before the Saxon invasion of around A.D. 800. It is the position rather than the buildings of the early monastic settlements which is so impressive. St Kevin's monastery at Glendalough has some interesting buildings, but the place is set apart by its atmosphere, which is conducive to a life of prayer and contemplation. An even more impressive monastic habitation is that of Skellig Michael off the coast of Kerry – a barren rock on which the monks lived in drystone huts like caves. It is surprising that the monks survived at all, since they must have lived lives of the utmost austerity. When the Vikings first arrived on Iceland they found that the only inhabitants were Irish hermits. The journey to Iceland in the superb Viking boats can have been no picnic, but how the monks got there in their frail curraghs, made of hide stretched over a wicker framework, is something of a miracle.

Irish scholarship and art were not limited to these islands. There were centres of Irish devotion, art and scholarship in Schaffhausen and St Gall in Switzerland. The monastery of Bobbio in North Italy was an Irish foundation and one of the Bishops of Salzburg was an Irishman. At a much later date, the teacher of the great scholar and theologian, St Thomas Aquinas, was an Irishman.

The sectarian strife in Northern Ireland has tended to make us somewhat sceptical of the religious claims of the two sides. Religion seems to be an excuse for civil war. However that may be, while I think the English are an intuitive people, the Irish are a deeply emotional and spiritual people. Their Catholicism is deeply devotional rather than scholarly and it is through their religion that their greatest achievements were made. This is sometimes slighted by the colder and more scholarly English Catholics. But it is Irish Catholicism that dominates the United States and Australia. Any list of the bishops of those countries – or of Great Britain, for that matter – will demonstrate by the names their Irish origins.

But to return to the period before the Viking invasions. Irish society of that period was organized on clan lines. The word 'king' is widely used, but they were, with some exceptions, only chieftains, perhaps 150 of them. They ruled over an agglomeration of family groups – often at war over cattle with other similar groups. At times a chieftain with more ability than his neighbours might build up a small kingdom or aspire to the honour of 'High King' of Ireland. But government was local, paternal and small-scale. The advent of Christianity introduced an entirely new element, the monastery, of which a number were founded in the very earliest days of missionary success. At first, as elsewhere, the leading ecclesiastics were bishops, but later they were the abbots of the larger foundations, who employed a bishop on their staff to carry out those ceremonies requiring celebration by a bishop. Later still the office of Abbot tended to become hereditary in the family of the founder, and contemporary opinion had no objection to lay abbots.

It was into this very ill-organized clan society that the Norsemen burst about the year 800. Apart from the kings and their following of lords and lawyers, there were the monasteries, which were the centres of art and religion. There were at that time no cities. Tara was a palace, not a city. There was no coinage: wealth was in cattle and inter-tribal war was a way of life, the prizes of which were cattle and slaves.

Chapter two

THE COMING OF THE VIKINGS

The impact of the Vikings on Ireland was quite different from their impact on England. To begin with, Ireland had not been invaded for many centuries, while England had sustained the Roman conquest, as well as many invasions by Continental peoples before that time. The organization of Irish society was in no way fitted for resistance to an enemy from without, and the Vikings were a most formidable enemy. Their two great assets were, first, immense courage, and, second, their boats, which represented a huge technical advance on any boat that had been built before that time. It is only recently that this factor has been fully appreciated as it is only recently that Viking ships have been raised from the sea in Scandinavia and fully studied. In the first place the Norsemen were looking for loot, which led them to voyages as far afield as Constantinople and Ireland. Raids on Ireland were aimed particularly at the monasteries, which were built mostly of wood, were not effectively defended and contained the treasures of Irish society. The precious metals were carried off, but not the books, which the Norsemen could not read. So except for some buried treasure most of what survives from the pre-Viking era are manuscripts.

Obviously the raids were purely destructive at first, but in time the Vikings formed settlements, and their permanent contribution to Ireland has been the cities they founded, such as Dublin, Wicklow, Waterford, Wexford, Cork and Limerick, all, naturally enough, on the sea, since the Vikings were a sea-faring race.

The Viking influence in Ireland was dominant for about two centuries, but did not lead to large-scale immigration, though there is still an area of Dublin called Oxmanstown, a corruption of 'The East Man's Town'. The Irish thought of the Vikings as coming from the east, while in England they were thought of as coming from the north. England being nearer Scandinavia than is Ireland, Norsemen tended to form permanent settlements there on a much larger scale than in Ireland.

The second great negative influence that distinguishes Irish history from English (the first being that Ireland was not colonized by Rome) is the Norman Conquest of 1066. This did not reach Ireland until a century later and then in a very different form. The Romans had given England a strong centralized government and so did the Normans. They imposed on England an iron-clad feudal system which gave autocratic powers to the sovereign. This rule was buttressed by their castles, erected at strategic points throughout the country and quite impregnable to any rebellious English. The Normans installed a system of law and the administration of justice of a more effective kind than was to be seen in Ireland for centuries.

By 1066 most of England except for the far west was populated by Anglo-Saxons of one kind or another: Jutes in Kent, Danes in the north-east, Norwegians – said to be from Ireland – in Cumberland, and so on. In Ireland the Viking settlements do not seem to have gone beyond the cities they founded. Whereas England had had a coinage imitating the staters of Alexander the Great since well before the Roman invasion, Dublin issued its first coins under the Vikings. They were very rough copies of pennies of Ethelred II, themselves very rough.

Though of course the various Viking communities in Europe became differentiated in time, in the early days there was some solidarity in feeling between the various lords. And it was the Vikings of Ireland who got in touch with personalities in England and acted as some sort of link between Ireland and England at that time. A Norse King of Dublin could aspire to be King of York and after the Norman Conquest the Irish Norsemen turned to the Anglo-Norman Archbishop of Canterbury for the consecration of their bishops.

But in general the warfare between petty kings in Ireland continued, in which the Norsemen participated. It is in this period that the Irish round towers which are a distinctively Irish contribution to architecture were built. At the threat of an attack, the community took refuge in the tower. It was high and served as a look-out and the entrance door was high off the ground. There the threatened monks or others could shelter until the enemy had moved on.

The great hero of this period in Irish history before the arrival of the Normans is Brian Boru, a chieftain of a minor group in the south-west of Ireland who defeated the Norsemen of Limerick and the Irish of Cashel and became High King of Ireland. He was finally killed in 1014 at the Battle of Clontarf, near Dublin, defeating invading Norsemen with the help of the Dublin Danes. This marked the end of the period of Norse invasions, and of the most promising attempt to set up an effective Irish monarchy.

The Norsemen had had a most damaging effect on the Irish monasteries, and Irish religion had had a monastic base. So in the eleventh and twelfth centuries efforts were made by succeeding Popes to reorganize religion in Ireland on an episcopal base and one looking to Rome. The leading figure in the Irish Church at this time was St Malachy, successively Abbot of Bangor (Co. Down), Bishop of Connor and Archbishop of Armagh. He worked closely with St Bernard of Clairvaux, who wrote his life.

St Bernard was one of the greatest personalities in Europe in his day, and it is rather touching to recall that St Malachy died in St Bernard's arms and was buried in his habit, while when St Bernard's time came he was buried in the habit of St Malachy.

In the first half of the twelfth century Cistercian monasteries were established, the independence of Armagh from Canterbury was confirmed by the Pope, and the Irish Church was provided with the four Archbishoprics the Catholic Church maintains to this day – Armagh, Dublin, Cashel and Tuam, These developments were not of purely ecclesiastical interest, as it was because of the desire of the Pope for reform in the Irish Church that he made a grant of Ireland to Henry II in 1155. As Dr Paisley says, Irish troubles are all the fault of the Pope: it was he who gave Ireland to Henry II. It has to be said that the Pope was Adrian IV, the only Englishman ever to become Pope.

Chapter three

THE NORMAN INVASION

The Pope felt not much could be done by purely ecclesiastical means to strengthen the Church in Ireland and the only temporal power with the necessary force was the King of England. Henry in turn might be interested in a principality for his younger son John.

Initially Henry took little real interest in Ireland, where inter-tribal warfare was continued as before, although the units were rather larger than in earlier times. In this somewhat fluid situation, Dermot MacMurrough, King of Leinster, was defeated and driven from his kingdom. Though he was an old man by the standards of his day, he did not take his defeat lying down. He journeyed to Bristol, which had close relations with Dublin. Bristol, then as later, was interested in the slave trade. At Bristol, MacMurrough seems to have obtained money and an introduction to Henry, who was in France, where he ruled a large area stretching from Rouen to Toulouse. When MacMurrough met the King, he found him more sympathetic than might have been expected. Henry gave him some money and a letter authorizing him to recruit what soldiers he could with whom to return to Ireland and regain his kingdom. Armed with this letter, he returned to Bristol but met with no enthusiasm for his cause. However, eventually he roused the interest of Strongbow, Earl of Pembroke, who had been on the losing side in the earlier history of Henry's reign and was quite willing to lead an expedition which might well put him back on the map. While Strongbow was obtaining Henry's consent to his taking part in the expedition, MacMurrough went home via South Wales, where he recruited some Welsh and Flemish mercenaries. With these he re-established himself in Leinster and waited for reinforcements. The first to arrive was one Robert Fitz-Stephen and a small band of knights and archers. This Fitz-Stephen was the founder of the great family of Fitzgerald who dominated Irish politics in later centuries and are still around as Dukes of Leinster.

Though the force was very small – only about 400 men – they had the advantage of more up-to-date military technology. The Irish traditionally fought with slings and axes, which were no sort of match for mounted knights in armour and certainly no match for the Welsh archers both mounted and unmounted.

Fitz-Stephen had sufficient success to encourage Strongbow to take the plunge with a larger force. He landed at Waterford in 1170 with a thousand men, encouraged by MacMurrough with the hope that with this force he could conquer the whole of Ireland. The *Annals of Ulster,* an ancient chronicle, says that with the arrival of Strongbow began all 'the woes of Ireland'. Up to that point wars had been petty affairs between rival Irish kings, but Strongbow's arrival was more in the nature of an invasion. In a few months he had had so much success that Henry began to fear he might soon have a rival feudal monarchy on his hands. Henry was also anxious to placate the Pope by taking some action over the Irish Church. He needed to do something, as the murder of St Thomas à Becket was a crime that called for some expiation.

On all these grounds Henry decided to take an expeditionary force to Ireland to assert his authority. The force was a very large one by contemporary standards, conveyed by 400 ships. It is always wise when using force to make sure the force is fully adequate. Henry's army was so overwhelming that it did not have to do any fighting and Henry received the homage of the Norman chiefs as well as that of most of the Irish kings. After a year in Ireland he returned home in 1172.

When speaking of those times it must be remembered that Henry was a Norman, not an Englishman, and that Norman French was spoken at his court. It was at this time that a number of the well-known Irish families first came to Ireland. Apart from the Fitzgeralds, the most notable are the Burkes, the Butlers and the de Courcys. Descended from the Flemish mercenaries of that date are the families of Roche and Prendergast.

It also has to be remembered that Henry's conquest of Ireland was very different from William's conquest of England a century earlier. William invaded England with a much larger force and in a very short time completely dominated and organized the whole country, while Scotland and Wales were sealed off. In Ireland Henry left behind no strong central administration and his writ did not run at all in the north-west. Another factor is the nature of the country. Ireland is now an open country with few woods, no forests and in some areas no trees. But at least until the seventeenth century it was difficult country for an invader, with much forest and widespread bogs. The Norman knights in particular were dependent on open country to be effective.

Henry's settlement of Ireland was short-lived and in 1177 he appointed his youngest son John to be Lord of Ireland. John was only ten at the time, and had three elder brothers, so Henry presumably intended Ireland to be a separate principality for John's permanent possession. It was from this period that a centre of government was set up in Dublin that has a continuous history down to our own day. John's government of Ireland was perhaps not as erratic as his government of England, but it marked the growth of the power of the Norman barons compared with that of the royal government. In any case John succeeded to the throne of England in 1199 and any idea of a separate principality of Ireland died at that time.

King John came back to Ireland in 1210 and by that time the nucleus of a royal administration had been set up in Dublin, beginning with the Exchequer. The King's supremacy was recognized by the various barons and Gaelic kings over about three-quarters of Ireland – roughly everything to the east of the Shannon and the Bann – but even this has to be qualified. There were areas, like the Dublin and Wicklow mountains, which maintained their semi-independence. In spite of King John's blunders in early youth his pacification of Ireland in 1210 seems to have been a success. When the English barons compelled him to sign Magna Carta in 1215, the Irish barons gave no trouble and remained loyal.

Though Ireland at this period was never really peaceful, the power of the Norman barons maintained a comparative peace in which the country prospered. Sheep-raising was taken up in a big way, new ports like Galway and Drogheda were established and market towns were founded all over the country. The ecclesiastical organization was strengthened and improved. Large numbers of religious houses dotted the countryside. The Franciscans were the favourites of the Gaelic areas, but most of the great orders of monks were established in Ireland.

Henry III succeeded his father when he was only nine years of age. This minority was not as disastrous as might have been expected, since succeeding English kings had evolved a system of absentee rule as they could not be in England and Gascony at the same time. In 1254 Ireland was granted to Edward, Henry's heir, but the intention was quite different from Henry II's grant of Ireland to John. On this occasion it was specifically stated that the grant was made so that the Lordship of Ireland should not be separated from the Crown of England. Moreover, John, though only a child, did come to Ireland, while Edward was also granted land in England and Wales, the Channel Islands and the whole of Gascony, and was much more interested in his French possessions than in Ireland. In fact no Lord of Ireland was to visit the country from 1210 until the reign of Richard II more than 150 years later. In Henry III's time stability was maintained under justiciars who remained in office for long periods, while in Edward's time a succession of short-lived justiciars was no help. But the trouble was not only neglect. Edward I's continuous wars were expensive and were financed in part by loans from Italian bankers, but even more by drawing huge sums from

Ireland. In fact the high point of English rule in Ireland in the Middle Ages was established in the reign of Henry III in the middle of the thirteenth century, and from then on a decline set in, leading, naturally, to a revival of Gaelic power and influence. In this period we see the first example of the treatment of the Irish that has bedevilled Anglo-Irish relations to the present day. With a powerful English administration installed on the island, it became impossible for the Irish to solve their own problems. Yet from the English point of view Ireland is normally a matter of peripheral interest and only comes into focus when help is needed at home or trouble arises.

The calls on Ireland persisted and increased until the Irish Exchequer was bankrupt. This in turn led to serious deterioration in the quality of the Dublin government. Not only did the Norman barons re-assert themselves, but the Gaelic chiefs saw opportunities in the decline of the central administration. It is from this time that we get the distinction made between the English and the Irish English. The former were born in England, the latter in Ireland. At times the Irish and the Irish English took sides against the English: at others it was all against all.

Under Edward II the situation deteriorated to such a point that the Ulster Irish established closer relations with the Scots and invited Edward Bruce, brother of the King of Scotland, to Ireland, where he was made 'King of Ireland'. This initiative led to much fighting and further deterioration in the Irish administration, which now became a drain on the English Exchequer. The damage done by the Bruce interlude was aggravated by the famine years of 1315–17, and some areas never really recovered.

In the early days of the Norman invasion the invaders had the advantage of new weapons and new tactics, but by the latter half of the thirteenth century, when the Dublin administration was in decline anyway, we have the influx of mercenary soldiers from Scotland, known as gallowglasses. This is a corruption of the Irish for 'foreign soldiers'. They came from the western islands of Scotland, spoke Gaelic and were fully a match for anything the Norman barons could bring against them.

At the beginning of the fourteenth century the King of Ulster sent a 'Remonstrance' (quoted in *The Lordship of Ireland in the Middle Ages*) addressed to Pope John XXII in the name of Gaelic Ireland. The Anglo-Irish, it said, were the English of the 'middle nation' – 'so different in character from the English of England and from other nations that with the greatest propriety they may be called a nation not of middle but of utmost perfidy.' Examples of their perfidy are quoted, such as 'lusting eagerly for our lands' and thus promoting endless war in which more than 50,000 of each nation were killed; inviting neighbours to banquets so as to murder them easily; or preaching the heresy that it was no more a sin to kill an Irishman than to kill a dog. It was impossible to live in peace with them.

For such is their arrogance and excessive lust to lord it over us and so great is our due and natural desire to throw off the unbearable yoke of their slavery and to recover our inheritance wickedly seized upon by them, that as there has not been hitherto, there cannot now be or ever henceforward be established, sincere goodwill between

them and us in this life. For we have a natural
hostility towards each other arising from the
mutual, malignant and incessant slaying of fathers,
brothers, nephews and other near relatives and
friends so that we can have no inclination to
reciprocal friendship in our time.

With the continued weakness of the Dublin government power passed to Norman barons in the provinces
and to Gaelic chiefs particularly in the north and west.
Many of the Normans, or English, as we may now call
them, became Gaelicized, even changing their names
to an Irish form. For instance, the Norman name of 'de
Angulo', after being translated into Irish as 'son of
Jocelin', and back into English, became the familiar
Irish name of Costello.

As time went on, English rule – at any rate effective
rule – became confined to Dublin and the Pale, which
was an area round Dublin that expanded or contracted
with the vagaries of war and politics. It tended to
extend north from Dublin, where there was open
country, while to the south were mountains, which
were harder to control.

Throughout the fourteenth century measures were
taken to prevent the corruption (as they saw it) of the
English by adopting Irish dress, customs and language,
but the trend of history was too strong and the decline
of English influence continued. How great this was
can be seen by the fact that even in Elizabeth I's reign
Irish was the language most commonly spoken in the
Pale.

In the reign of Edward III efforts were made to
assert the royal authority, but money was lacking and

Edward was more concerned with French affairs than with Irish. So the area dominated by Gaelic chiefs tended to grow, as did the area occupied by 'English rebels', as they were called. With lack of any effective central authority the various Anglo-Norman families fell to fighting each other. It is of these people that the Irish Council said in 1399 that 'the English Nations who are rebels in all parts of the country such as the Butlers, Poers, Geraldines, Daltons, Barretts and Dillons are not amenable to the law, and though they wish to be called gentlemen are in truth nothing but sturdy robbers.' (*The Lordship of Ireland in the Middle Ages.*)

By the end of the century an additional source of weakness had shown itself. Many of the more important landowners were absentees, which gave additional opportunities to any disorderly elements. This was a problem by no means limited to the fourteenth century, as we shall see.

Another important factor was the Black Death of 1349–50, which depopulated Ireland in the same way as it had depopulated much of Europe. But in Ireland it naturally affected most the towns, which were the centres of English influence. So the result was still further to weaken the English control of the island.

Richard II visited Ireland on at least two occasions with a large army. The force was so large that, as in Henry II's day, no serious fighting was necessary. But in the conditions of that day to force the various rebellious English and Irish chiefs to do homage had no lasting effect. Much money had been spent but there was no follow-through.

A Tudor commentator, Gerrard, said of medieval

Ireland, 'The quiet estate of the land began to decay because the English degenerating became Irish.' The truth of the matter was that the English kings, with their preoccupation nearer home with Wales, Scotland and France, had not the resources, even if they had had the wish, to effect the complete conquest of Ireland. The royal administration in Dublin, left to itself, had some difficulty in holding on even to the Pale, which tended to comprise the counties of Dublin, Kildare, Meath and Louth.

In the fifteenth century, under the Lancastrian kings, the situation remained the same, only worse. The royal exchequer was always desperately short of money and Ireland had a very low priority except when the question of security was raised. How low a priority can be seen by the fact that the Lieutenant of Gascony in the middle of the fifteenth century received £36,000 a year, while the Lieutenant of Ireland was given the impossible task of making do on £2,000. The Channel Islands, and above all Calais, fared enormously better than Ireland. More was spent on the Scottish and Welsh marches than on Ireland. Even the meagre stipend payable to the Irish Lieutenant was often not paid, and it became increasingly difficult to get any Englishman of standing to take the job. But the same argument did not apply to the Anglo-Norman magnates of Ireland, who could use the office of Lieutenant for their own aggrandizement. And in fact the office of Lieutenant became a bone of contention between the Butlers, the Talbots and the Fitzgeralds, ending with the triumph of the last. The eighth Earl of Kildare, Garret Fitzgerald, virtually ruled Ireland at the end of the fifteenth century, when the English were busy with the aftermath of the Wars of the Roses. It is interesting that another Garret Fitzgerald is a minister of the present Irish Government.

Though the central exchequer was bankrupt and the king's authority limited to the Pale, so called from 1446 and an imitation of the Calais Pale, the country enjoyed a rising standard of prosperity. Wars in Ireland in the Middle Ages were not necessarily very destructive.

The Fitzgerald rule in Ireland continued until 1535, when the rebellious tenth Earl of Kildare was defeated at Maynooth by the royal forces and a new era began, as it was at this time that Henry VIII broke with the Pope with even more momentous consequences for Ireland than for the rest of the king's dominions.

Hitherto England's relationship with Ireland since the Norman invasion of 1169 had reflected the desire of the English kings to prevent Ireland being a security risk. This desire had not been sufficient to lead them to attempt the conquest of Ireland and the organization of English rule, so that there was continued warfare between rival Irish chieftains and Norman barons without any decisive result. The Anglo-Norman families became in many ways Irish and the Gaelic chiefs no doubt became Anglicized to some extent. At least up to this point there was no difference of religion to complicate a confused situation.

Chapter four

THE PLANTATIONS

With the end of the fifteenth century we enter something more like the modern world, though Ireland in 1500 was more like England at an earlier date. In 1515, early in Henry VIII's reign, there appeared an official document called 'The State of Ireland and Plan for its Reformation stated: And first of all to make his Grace understand that there may be more than 60 counties, called regions in Ireland, inhabited with the King's Irish enemies: some regions as big as a shire, some more, some less, unto a little: some as big as half a shire and some a little less: where reigneth more than 60 chief captains that liveth only by the sword and obeyeth to no other temporal persons but only to himself that is strong.'

At that date, in so far as there was a central government at all, it was in the hands of the Earl of Kildare and so remained until 1535. The fundamental change in Irish affairs took place in the same decade when Henry repudiated the supremacy of the Pope and dissolved the monasteries. Their extensive lands in Ireland were taken over by the big landlords, whether Norman or Gaelic. In this as in much else the Tudors were more efficient and ruthless rulers than those who had gone before them. Moreover they had no internal dissensions to distract them at home, nor were they burdened with responsibilities for big French possessions.

32

In dealing with the Ireland of that time it has to be remembered that there were few roads, no reliable maps, and that the government in London was handicapped by a lack of reliable information on which to base any policy. Moreover, the areas under Gaelic control were protected by thick and almost impenetrable woods. English sixteenth-century governments soon grasped the idea that to send an army to Ireland and exact homage from the leading figures in the country provided no lasting solution to anything. If English rule was to have meaning, it must proceed by building roads and organizing the countryside into counties on English lines. Furthermore, as the organization proceeded, fortifications must be built to protect the area organized, and colonists must above all be encouraged by grants of land to come to Ireland and occupy the pacified area. So a beginning was made with the counties of Leix and Offaly, renamed Queen's County and King's County after Mary Tudor and her husband, Philip of Spain. These are the counties immediately to the west and south of Kildare, and were the natural extension to the Pale.

The dissolution of the monasteries was carried through without too much trouble – the losers were the poor and the Irish, the gainers the rich and the powerful. The repudiation of Rome was quite another matter and was, as we know, never accepted by the Gaelic Irish. In any case the Pope had always played a more active part in Irish affairs than in English ones, where the Vatican had always acted through the monarchy.

The later years of the sixteenth century were dominated by the crushing of the rebellion of James Fitz-

Maurice Fitzgerald, cousin of the Earl of Desmond, in the south-west and the subsequent revolt of the O'Neills in Ulster, though the latter rebellion had repercussions all over the country. The final defeat of the O'Neills and the flight of the two O'Neill earls is often taken to mark the end of the old order in Ireland.

Edmund Spenser, the poet, was secretary to the Lord Deputy, Lord Grey of Wilton. He was a settler and took part in the crushing of the Desmond rebellion in Munster in 1583. He reports the scene at the end:

> Out of every corner of the woods and glens they came creeping forth upon their hands, for their legs would not bear them: they looked like anatomies of death: they spoke like ghosts crying out of their graves: they did eat the dead carrions, happy where they could find them: yea and one another soon after, insomuch as the very carcasses they spared not to scrape out of their graves.

After his own house at Kilcoleman had been burned by the rebels, he considered "How then? Should the Irish have been quite rooted out? That were too bloody a course: and yet their continual rebellious deeds deserve little better." (From O'Brien, *A Concise History of Ireland*.)

The Desmond rebellion was to have been helped by a Spanish and Italian force of 600 men which landed in Kerry on the Dingle peninsula. It was beleaguered by Lord Grey and surrendered, whereupon 'certain bands' under the young Raleigh (another settler) were put in, who killed off the prisoners. These early colonists seem to illustrate some of the worst aspects of colonial forces anywhere.

The Gaelic order – together with such of the older English settlers as had accommodated themselves too well to that order – was now doomed, through the convergence on it of overwhelming forces. Renaissance ideas of order and civility, and zeal for the Reformed faith, were among these forces, but the most urgent drive came from elsewhere, allied with these but distinct: the nationalism of a menaced England. Henry VIII had himself proclaimed King of Ireland in 1541, but did not securely establish English rule. The Protestant reforms carried out under Edward VI had not been enforced in Ireland and, under Mary, England's control over Ireland further weakened. Thus on the accession of Elizabeth to an insecure and threatened throne, Ireland presented an opening to the enemies of the Queen of England, and of the Reformation. To pacify it was felt to be a necessity of national survival: and pacification required the destruction of the Gaelic order whose forms of liberty were, in English eyes, anarchy.

Elizabeth herself had no enthusiasm for conquering Ireland, a costly and discouraging task – but her situation required this to be done. The Reformed faith had made hardly any progress among either the Irish or the Old English, as they were called. The devoted missionaries of the counter-Reformation, on the other hand, found ready ears, and among their themes were the illegitimacy of Elizabeth and the duty of deposing her. It became necessary for Elizabeth's generals to fight four wars in Ireland: all of them involved the possibility, and the last two the reality, of intervention by England's Continental enemies.

A pattern had now established itself that was

to prove enduring: Catholic Ireland dominated by the superior force of Protestant England. Religion hardened, sharpened and preserved national animosities. Among the Irish a persecuted Church fanned the resentment of a conquered people: the English were heretics, their power was illegitimate, rebellion against them lawful, their enemies were the friends of Ireland and of the Faith. It was a vicious circle. English consciousness of these sentiments produced strong measures, thus intensifying the Irish feelings at the root of the original feeling of insecurity, and creating the need for still further strong measures.

The best answer, from an English point of view, was to uproot the hostile native population, and replace them with loyal Protestants from England, Scotland and Wales: the method of settlements recommended by Machiavelli in *The Prince*. Raleigh had tried and failed in Munster, Queen Mary in the Midlands. The Flight of the Earls, however, cleared the way for a new plantation, this time in much more propitious conditions. The estates of the earls were declared forfeit to the Crown and an effort was made, which was partially successful, to have a large territory – most of Ulster – settled from England and Scotland. If this policy had been consistently and generally applied, England could have solved its Irish problem. But in fact no policy was consistently applied over any long period: Ireland's affairs received only intermittent attention, perfunctory except in times of real danger. (*A Concise History of Ireland.*)

The attitude of the native Irish is wonderfully described by a Catholic bishop writing in 1617:

> They have been deprived of weapons but are in a temper to fight with nails and heels, and to tear their oppressors with their teeth. Since they see themselves excluded from all hopes of restitution or compensation, and are so constituted that they would rather starve upon husks at home, than fare sumptuously elsewhere. They will fight for their altars and hearths, and rather seek a bloody death near the sepulchres of their fathers than be buried as exiles in unknown earth. (*A Concise History of Ireland.*)

By the 1630s large numbers of Scots were planted in Ulster, and Wentworth, Earl of Strafford, whose motto was 'Thorough', was sent by Charles I to impose an effective government on the country. Various interpretations have been put on his rule of Ireland, but it was certainly thorough; it was ruthless and it was intended to make Ireland a bastion of political support for Charles. Under his control Connacht was planted, but his arbitrary rule built up fierce resentment among the various groups of which the Irish population was then composed – the English in the Pale, the planters, the Old English who were Catholics, the Old English who were Protestants and the native Irish who remained Catholic. Ill-feeling on a big scale led to rebellion in 1641 which was in part related to the English Civil War, and which rumbled on until finally crushed by Cromwell in 1653. The rising originated in Ulster, the scene of the largest and most recent plantations, and was supported by the Old English Catholics and the native Irish throughout Ireland. In 1649 Charles I was beheaded and Cromwell came to Ireland. In the subsequent fighting the Catholic powers of the continent did not intervene and the rebels had no chance against Cromwell's Ironsides. What is still remembered about the four years of fighting is the ruthlessness of Cromwell and his soldiers, particularly the massacre of prisoners at the siege of Drogheda, and even worse at the siege of Wexford. In both cases the Irish losses were around 2,000, while at Wexford those of the Parliamentary troops were trifling. When I was young in Ireland 'the curse of Cromwell' still had considerable emotional and political force. Actually the seventeenth century was a pretty ruthless age and it does not seem that Cromwell was any more ruthless than his opponents or than was customary in contemporary warfare. But the better propagandists were the Irish.

At the end of the fighting the policy was to push the Irish into the rocky and boggy area west of the Shannon, while the good land was reserved for English and Scottish settlers, particularly the soldiers of Cromwell's army, whose political reliability could be assumed. But labour was needed on the English estates, so that what actually happened was that the good land was taken from the Irish and owned mainly by English landowners, while the native Irish remained to some extent as labourers, and to some extent were pushed aside on to inferior land the settlers did not want. This was the pattern all over Ireland except in eastern Ulster where the land was held by Scottish Presbyterian peasants. It was at this time, in the middle of the seventeenth century, that the pattern was set for the social and economic life of the Irish countryside that remained intact until the latter half of the last century. It was estimated that in 1641 Catholics still held three-fifths of the land in Ireland but by 1665 it had fallen to one-fifth, mostly in the far west. By 1800 this proportion had fallen still further to 8 per cent.

Under the Restoration and the reign of Charles II no great changes were made, but the final test of strength in Ireland came with the arrival of James II in 1689. He had been defeated and banished from England in the 'Glorious Revolution' of 1688 and had fled to France. From there he came to Ireland where his general, Richard Talbot, Earl of Tyrconnell, with a Catholic army, controlled all Ireland except Londonderry and Enniskillen. But an English fleet relieved Londonderry and William III landed at Carrickfergus and defeated James II at the Battle of the Boyne, an event still widely celebrated in the Six Counties, as we know from our television screens. This has become a great propaganda event rather than a military one. James was a half-hearted commander and his troops had not the equipment of the English army under William. In the long run – even if James had won the Battle of the Boyne – the result would have been the same. It is an interesting sidelight on the unrealistic quality of Vatican politics at that time that, James II having been recognized as the legitimate king, Irish Catholics were still instructed to pray for his son as James III until 1766.

The final defeat of the Catholic forces under James led to the passing of the penal laws, many of which were to remain in force until the nineteenth century. These laws were partly to keep down a conquered but

39

politically dangerous people but partly to ensure the transfer of even more land into Protestant hands. The motive was not racist; the laws were motivated by religion and greed, but the effect was much the same. Even in our own day in Ireland a Catholic–Protestant marriage would be regarded as an act of betrayal by the friends of both parties.

But to return to the penal laws – no Catholic could sit in Parliament or vote in Parliamentary elections. They were excluded from the professions and no Catholic could keep a school. A Catholic might not even send his children abroad to be educated. Complicated rules were made over the ownership of land, the effect of which was that most of the land that was still in Catholic hands passed to Protestants. As was true of so much of Anglo-Irish relations, the laws were ferocious, the implementation of them capricious. No policy in Ireland was ever carried through to its logical conclusion.

In England, the Revolution of 1688 had made the King dependent on Parliament, which he was compelled to summon at regular intervals. The Bill of Rights, however, did not apply to Ireland, which was governed by the King and council in Dublin, though the English Parliament claimed an overriding power in Irish affairs. There was an Irish Parliament, but in the first three-quarters of the eighteenth century it was the creature of the government. The thirty-two Irish counties returned two members each, and a number of boroughs had one or two representatives, bringing the total up to about 300. The Irish House of Commons was elected at the beginning of a new reign and remained until the King's death. The English

House of Lords claimed the right to hear appeals from Irish judges. The Lord Lieutenant was resident in Ireland for six months every two years during the sitting of the Irish parliament. In the interval the government was substantially in the hands of three officials who undertook to keep a subservient parliamentary majority in return for dispensing royal patronage. The officials were the Primate, the Lord Chancellor and the Speaker of the House of Commons. Occasionally popular opinion made itself felt, as with Dean Swift and his agitation over Wood's Ha'pence in 1723, but in general the government control of the country was absolute.

It was not only the native Irish who had grievances – so had the Scottish settlers in Ulster. While their Scottish brethren from 1707 sent members to Westminster and had their Presbyterian Church recognized as the Established Church of Scotland, the Irish Presbyterians suffered from most of the same disabilities as the Catholics.

Conor Cruise O'Brien in his *Concise History* quotes an Irish Protestant writing in the early part of the eighteenth century:

> We seemed strange and remote to the English, like a people setting up for ourselves. They looked on us as at a distance. There was no one to explain the difference between the English and Irish inhabitants: and one impression (of all of them together) was that they were a disloyal and turbulent people, who could only be rendered harmless as long as they were disabled by poverty.

At times I think that some part of this view of Ireland and the Irish still lingers in certain quarters in London.

Chapter five

IRELAND SUBJUGATED: THE COMING OF UNION

In the latter half of the eighteenth century two events brought about a change in the political climate of Ireland. The first was the accession of George III, and the second was the revolt of the American colonies in 1776. The troops garrisoning Ireland were sent to America and there was a considerable fear of a Spanish or French invasion. The result was what was called the 'Constitution of 1782'. It was no new constitution, but as a result of the patriotic eloquence of Flood and Grattan, two Irish Protestant M.P.s, the penal laws were modified and Ireland had a Parliament which had some powers and a Viceroy in permanent residence. The administration was entirely in the hands of the Government in London.

Partly owing to the lifting of restrictions on Irish trade, this was a period of prosperity in Ireland, marked by the erection of the splendid eighteenth-century buildings which are such a distinguishing mark of Dublin's architecture to this day. It was also in the eighteenth century that Irish silversmiths produced some of the finest work in Europe and by the end of the century Irish cut glass was to set a standard still unsurpassed. The buildings and the furniture were designed for the Protestant aristocracy. The growing political ferment was led by Protestants, though it had some Catholic support.

The unrest at this time was due partly to the inadequacy of the government of Ireland and in part to the competition for land. This again was due not only to the land taken by the planters and the settlers but also to a rapidly rising population. The reasons for this are not clear; the population estimates in the absence of a census have to be treated with caution. But it does appear that the Irish population between 1767 and the end of the century doubled from $2\frac{1}{2}$ million to 5 million – about what it is today.

Ireland in the earlier years of the century had been governed like a colony and in fact it set a pattern for colonial governments in the succeeding century. The American revolution was of a kind with which the Protestant Ascendancy could sympathize. People much like themselves were seeking control of their own affairs without meddling from London. The French Revolution of 1789, however, was a totally different matter. While it might appeal to the downtrodden Catholic masses and the Presbyterian farmers, it could only present the gravest threat to the ruling classes – a threat both to their power and their property.

Edmund Burke – another Protestant Irishman – contended that the safest course was to make concessions to the Catholics, and some concessions were made in 1793, but the progress of the war with France and the efforts of Wolfe Tone, another Protestant Irishman, to bring about, through a movement called the United Irishmen, an independent republic on French principles inevitably led to repression. This was to be the pattern of British policy right down to our own day – alternating bouts of conciliation and repression. Either policy might have succeeded: failure is the only possible consequence of the alternation.

The United Irishmen did not spring up unheralded.

They had been preceded by other secret societies and in fact in the decades up to the 1790s there had been outrages of various kinds throughout the country. In the 1770s and subsequently there had been intermittent warfare in Ulster between the Protestant Peep O'Day Boys and the Catholic Defenders. It was in 1795 after a skirmish in County Armagh between these groups that the victorious Protestants founded the Orange Society, of which much more was to be heard.

Reminiscent of Lord Randolph Churchill's remark nearly a century later of 'playing the Orange card' is this statement in 1797 of the military commander in Dungannon, announcing that he was starting a search for unregistered arms: 'And this I do, not so much with a hope to succeed to any extent, as to increase the animosity between the Orangemen and the United Irishmen. Upon that animosity depends the safety of the centre counties of the North.'

The policy of military repression was first applied in 1797 in Ulster. After the arrest of many leading United Irishmen and the capture and death of the popular hero Lord Edward Fitzgerald, widespread rebellion broke out. There were two main centres, of which the Ulster one was substantially Presbyterian, while the Wexford one was purely Catholic. The rebellion was defeated partly by the Volunteers, who included Catholics as well as Protestants in their ranks. When the rising had been crushed, help arrived from France, accompanied by Wolfe Tone who was captured and later committed suicide in prison. The rebellion had been unorganized, and was put down with great brutality. In mitigation of this fact it has to be remembered that England at this time was fighting for her life against the revolutionary armies of France.

W. B. Yeats, the great Irish poet, said in 1923 that there were 'Four Bells – four deep tragic notes in Irish history'. The first was the Flight of the Earls in 1607 which marked the end of the old Gaelic order; the second was the Battle of the Boyne in 1690; the third was the Rebellion of 1798; and the last was the death of Parnell in 1891.

Even during the '98 rebellion William Pitt, the English Prime Minister, was considering the Union of England and Ireland and the abolition of the Irish Parliament. His motives were partly the search for security in wartime and partly the belief that a common parliament for the two countries, coupled with Catholic emancipation, would be the answer to the problem of maintaining law and order in Ireland and reconciling to each other the various elements in the Irish population. In 1801 Pitt created the Union of the English and the Irish Parliaments.

In long retrospect the abolition of Grattan's Parliament has seemed to many a disastrous political move forced through by corruption of every kind. The Irish Parliament from 1782 to 1800, however, was only seen in this favourable light when it had long ceased to exist. In fact the 300 members of the Irish Parliament became 100 Irish M.P.s at Westminster with an appropriate addition of Irish peers to the House of Lords. These representations had a substantial say in the affairs of the United Kingdom, though a less direct say in Irish affairs. But the Irish Parliament had been entirely under the control of the British Government, so the change could reasonably be represented as a change for the better. Unfortunately, a key element in Pitt's policy was that there should be Catholic emancipation. Though much of the anti-Catholic legislation had been repealed or allowed to lapse, much remained. Full emancipation ran into difficulties with George III, who said it would be a violation of his Coronation Oath. It subsequently ran into opposition from powerful Protestant elements on both sides of the Irish Sea and had to be abandoned. It was finally passed in 1829 under very different circumstances.

The Westminster Parliament of 1800 was the unreformed Parliament complete with rotten boroughs, and Irish representation, mostly of cities and boroughs, was dominated by important families or by the government. Opportunities for the expression of popular opinion were rare, and Emmet's rising in Dublin in 1803 served no immediate or practical purpose, though he contributed to the nationalist propaganda of later times.

The practical effects of the Union were that the list of grievances due to the bad government of Ireland grew longer. Redress was harder to obtain, since Irish affairs were a minor preoccupation of the British House of Commons. Ireland had its own Exchequer, but under the new arrangement had to contribute two-seventeenths of total United Kingdom expenditure. This was a heavy burden for a poor country, saddled for fifteen years with this share of the cost of the Napoleonic Wars.

In the eighteenth century the Presbyterian counties of Ulster had been as revolutionary as any of the Catholic areas, but with the Union their commercial and industrial interests became bound up with those of England. The freer trade which was created by the Union caused the rise of prosperity of Belfast; a prosperity based on the linen industry in the first place and subsequently on shipbuilding and the ancillary trades connected therewith.

So from 1800 the Anglican Protestants of the South saw in the Union the great bastion of their political power, while the Presbyterians of the North saw in the Union the whole basis of their commercial prosperity. The Catholics on the other hand, as democratic ideas began to come into fashion, realized that the Catholics at Westminster could never be more than a minority, while in an Irish Parliament elected on any basis that allowed the Catholics a vote, the Catholics would inevitably be in a majority. Hence the agitation for an Irish Parliament – not the Parliament of Grattan, to which Catholics were not admitted, but a parliament which in its membership gave due weight to the Catholic majority in the country.

Part of the opposition to the Union had been the very natural reluctance of important social and commercial elements in Dublin to see their city deprived in considerable measure of its importance as a capital. And in fact all the fine buildings that make Dublin such a fine town today date from before 1800.

Chapter six

O'CONNELL AND CATHOLIC EMANCIPATION

The next great figure in Irish history is Daniel O'Connell, the Liberator. He came of a family of native Irish landowners in County Kerry. Though he spoke English in his family circle, notably with his uncle Maurice, the head of the family, he also spoke fluent Irish. He was educated in France at St Omer and Douai between 1791 and 1793, when the revolutionary fervour in France was at its height. In 1794 he came back to London, where he read for the bar and immersed himself in the liberal and radical literature of the period. He was called to the Irish Bar in 1798 and was an active politician until his death in 1847. He was strongly opposed to violence and joined a Yeomanry Corps of lawyers to uphold law and order at the time of the Emmet rebellion.

In subsequent years Catholic influence was diminished by differences within their ranks: also by the differing views of Grattan within the House of Commons and O'Connell outside. A Catholic Relief Bill did indeed pass the House of Commons in 1821, but was rejected by the House of Lords. At this period it would seem that Catholic opinion was not antagonistic to the British connection. When George IV visited Ireland in 1821 he had a wildly favourable reception. The English did not return this enthusiasm.

Apart from O'Connell's activities, which we shall

come to in a moment, an important development in the early years of the nineteenth century was the re-organization and reform of the Catholic Church in Ireland. This had been begun in 1795 when the great Catholic seminary was established at Maynooth with a grant from the British government. From this period the priesthood was better educated, better trained and drawn from a wider social spectrum of Irish society. It was perhaps for this reason that from about 1830 the priesthood took an increasingly active part in nationalist politics.

To return to Daniel O'Connell: his success, apart from his native eloquence, depended on two new ideas: the 'Catholic Rent', a political subscription of one penny per month; and the mass meeting. The first provided the necessary funds, and the second gave his agitation for Catholic emancipation enormous propaganda impetus. The Rent not only provided the cash, but it also gave the peasantry a sense of involvement in a campaign which would benefit the Catholic professional classes but not the working classes except in the long term. O'Connell's movement really took off in 1824.

Catholic emancipation was viewed favourably by a number of the leading English politicians, but they had to contend with George IV and with the House of Lords. Hopes were raised when Canning and subsequently Goderich became Prime Ministers, as they were known to be favourable, but the Wellington–Peel administration took over in 1828, pledged to oppose emancipation. This provided O'Connell with the great moment of his career. In the formation of the new Government the M.P. for Clare, one Vesey-Fitzgerald, was appointed to the Cabinet and according to the rules at that time had to seek re-election. He was a good member, supported by the Clare gentry and himself sympathetic to the Catholic cause. After some hesitation O'Connell decided to stand against him in the by-election and won easily. When he reached the Bar of the House of Commons he refused to take the declaration against transubstantiation and the anti-Catholic Oath of allegiance and was not allowed to take his seat. But the intense excitement of the Clare election and its aftermath left the British government in no doubt that the question had now become Catholic Emancipation or rebellion, in which the Irish would have had much English sympathy. O'Connell's brinkmanship won the day: the Duke of Wellington and Sir Robert Peel persuaded the King and the House of Lords that Catholic Emancipation could no longer be deferred and so in April 1829 the act received the King's signature and an important political milestone had been passed.

Emancipation had been achieved as the result of organized mass protest, leading, if necessary, to Civil War. This was the first occasion in Anglo-Irish politics on which the British Government yielded to the threat of force what it would not yield to persuasion – a disastrous lesson was learnt by the Irish and one which still dominates Anglo-Irish politics today.

The effect of Emancipation was to give the Irish masses some sense of self-respect. Under O'Connell's inspired leadership they had really achieved something. But the measure that brought in Emancipation increased the qualification in Ireland for the vote and thus disfranchised the great majority of the poorer voters. The lot of the peasantry was unaltered. The people who gained were the Catholic middle classes, who were now able to play a greater part in the politics of their country. However, up to 1919 the administration was kept firmly in the hands of the Protestant majority and only a few posts, for appearance's sake, were allotted to 'Castle Catholics' as they were known – Dublin Castle being the seat of the Irish government.

The success of O'Connell's campaign for Emancipation was noted by other agitators and set the pattern for the activities of the Chartists and the Anti-Corn Law League. O'Connell seems to have thought that he had discovered a universally effective political weapon. What had won Emancipation could win Home Rule, or Repeal as it was then called, and he started to work towards it.

The face of English politics was transformed by the great Reform Bill of 1832 which took representation away from the rotten boroughs, like Old Sarum, which had no inhabitants but returned two members to Parliament, and gave it to the great industrial towns of the north and the midlands. This Act did not apply to Ireland; the corresponding Act of 1833 allotted a few extra seats to the counties but the pocket boroughs remained. The Governments that took office after 1832 were not very different from those before that date, though important legislation on the Poor Law and other matters was passed by the Whig Government, supported as it was by O'Connell for most of the time. Long wrangles took place over Irish Church matters which are not really relevant to my purpose. Legislation was passed on the Irish municipalities and the Poor Law.

In 1841 Sir Robert Peel became Prime Minister. In a letter to Lord Ellenborough he said, 'We have that great standing evil, which counterbalances all good, the State of Ireland.' His Government included no less than four ex-Chief Secretaries of Ireland, one of the four being himself. So, unlike most other periods, the British Cabinet when discussing Ireland at least knew what it was talking about. In further comments of the same period which are as applicable now as they were then he observed that the English had conspicuously failed in either Ireland or Canada to establish a working relationship with the Catholic Church. His other remark was that the fundamental weakness in the maintaining of law and order in Ireland was the inability to secure the ordinary administration of justice, since its basic institution – the jury system – rested on a presumption of identity between the jurymen and the state which in Ireland did not exist.

The administration of Ireland at that time was conducted by a resident Viceroy, usually a wealthy peer, and a Chief Secretary who was responsible for Irish affairs in the House of Commons. The Viceroy was more active than the Sovereign in London and in any case had a known political complexion: the Chief Secretary had some of the attributes of an Irish Prime Minister. Under Peel's administration the Viceroy was Lord de Grey, an ultra-conservative of a rather emotional type, while the Chief Secretary was Lord Eliot, who held a courtesy title as the eldest son of Lord St Germans. Eliot was much more liberal and less authoritarian than the Viceroy and was in general supported by Peel. On the other hand the Viceroy was supported by the Under-Secretary. It was not an arrangement that could be expected to work smoothly at a time of violent agitation. Anything one reads about Peel shows him to have been a great Prime Minister – with Gladstone and Pitt, perhaps one of the three great Prime Ministers of the last century. Though O'Connell castigated him as 'Orange Peel' he was not a reactionary, but knew he was responsible not only for Ireland but also for England and Scotland, which were in the throes of the industrial revolution and in 1842 were to face one of the worst years of the century for mass unemployment and acute social distress.

Agitation for Repeal within the Parliamentary system was getting O'Connell nowhere, but in 1843 the movement took on fresh life in the Irish countryside, subscriptions looked up, the Archbishop of Tuam joined the movement at the head of a hundred of his priests. Thomas Davis's paper *The Nation* took up the cause; giant meetings were held: one at Tara was said to have been attended by a million people – certainly exaggerated, although reasonable observers estimated the attendance at something like half that number. The Viceroy was all for repressive measures, but Peel was in the difficulty that he was faced in England with a similar agitation by the Anti-Corn Law League. He could hardly take punitive measures against O'Connell without doing the same in England against the Anti-Corn Law League and to clamp down on both at once was hardly practicable.

In October, O'Connell announced a monster meeting at Clontarf, the scene of the great victory of Brian Boru. He had been promising the early success of his Repeal movement. However, he had got himself into a position where to press on would have meant armed rebellion and to retreat would mean the disintegration of his movement. He was 68 and no believer in armed insurrection. He called off the Clontarf meeting and this really marked the close of his career. In the case of Catholic Emancipation the British Government were prepared to yield to the threat of war: in the case of Repeal they were not. There was, however, this to be said: the Repeal had brought Irish affairs to the attention of English politicians of all parties, as Chartism and the Anti-Corn Law League had done for what was called the 'Condition of England' question.

In 1844 Peel circulated a paper to his Cabinet in which he enunciated the following views – far more enlightened than those of later Conservative Prime Ministers:

As long as Ireland remained disaffected, the United Kingdom was embarrassed in its foreign relations and vulnerable in time of war. Ireland would remain a source of danger until it was efficiently governed. It could not be efficiently governed as long as Irish Courts and juries were useless as the foundation of law and order. They would continue to be useless until the professional middle classes in Ireland identified themselves with the state. They would not so identify themselves until they and their church were given political and cultural as well as legal equality. This full equality could only come if professionally, educationally and socially they were given the same opportunities as Protestants. To achieve this, after centuries of inferiority, Parliament and the taxpayer must come to the assistance of the Irish Catholics both lay and clerical. (From *Sir Robert Peel,* by Norman Gash.)

Apart from the Law and Order question, and it has to be remembered that at this date in the early 'forties the British garrison in Ireland was larger than that in India, Peel was concerned with the lot of the Irish peasant. Having decided to have an inquiry conducted into the matter he was interested to receive a sensible letter from the Earl of Devon, who was both an English and an Irish landlord. He was appointed Chairman of the Commission, which was a small one, made up, it is true, of landlords, but landlords of an enlightened character. At least they had experience of the subject they were investigating, unlike a similar commission today which would be packed with lawyers, professors and trade union secretaries. It is this Devon report which is the basis of our knowledge of Irish conditions in the countryside in the months immediately before the Famine.

The Report stated that the principal cause of Irish misery was the bad relations between landlord and tenant. Ireland was a conquered country, the Irish peasant a dispossessed man: his landlord an alien conqueror. There was no paternalism, such as existed in England, no hereditary loyalty or feudal tie. 'Confiscation is their common title,' said the Earl of Clare, the Tory Lord Chancellor, speaking of Irish landlords, 'and from the first settlements they have been hemmed in on every side by the original inhabitants of the island, brooding over their discontent in sullen indignation.'

'It would be impossible adequately to describe',

55

stated the Devon Commission in its report, 'the priva-
tions which the Irish labourer and his family habitually
and silently endure. In many districts their only food
is the potato, their only beverage water: their cabins
are seldom a protection against the weather: a bed
or a blanket is a rare luxury: and in nearly all, their
pig and a manure heap constitute their only property.'

Owing to a rapidly growing population the competition for land was desperate and rents in Ireland
were very high – much higher than in England.
Though the practice was uneconomic, farms were con-
stantly divided and sub-divided among members of a
family, as the possession of a small plot of ground was
the only means of assuring a supply of food. The farms
were so small that there was no demand for agricultural
labourers and no industry to supply work in the towns.
Such Poor Law legislation as existed was designed to
make the Irish pay for their own paupers and refrain
from letting them come to England. Additional to the
evil of extreme poverty, Irish tenants, except in Ulster
where they had certain rights, had no security of tenure,
and any improvements accrued to the benefit of the
landlord. Most of the landlords were Protestants, but
Catholic landlords, such as there were, were no less
rapacious. A particular evil of the system was that
many landlords were absentee. Some of them had only
once visited the property from which they drew their
income. In other cases the landlord had never seen his
property. The management was made over to a resident bailiff, or the property was sub-let, and it was
the middleman – sometimes several layers of them –
who were the most rapacious of all.

In the 1840s Irish poverty and Irish misery appalled

the traveller. The Frenchman de Beaumont found in Ireland the extreme of human misery, worse than the Negro in his chains. The German traveller Kohl wrote that no mode of life in Europe could seem pitiable after one had seen Ireland.

This appalling state of affairs was due both to the greed and callousness of the landlords and the ineptitude of British governments, but the third factor was the huge rise in the population. It is calculated that between 1767 and 1800 the population doubled to 5 million, while at the census of 1841 the total was 8,175,000, and this is thought to be below the real figure. Any government would have been hard put to it to cope with a population explosion of that magnitude, but the British government seems not to have been aware of the size of the problem. The reasons for this population increase are not really understood. No one can pretend that in the Ireland of that day hygiene or medical attention showed any improvement on previous centuries and a diet of potatoes would not strike one as particularly beneficial. The English population over the same period also showed a marked increase under circumstances that were entirely different. The concentration of population was greatest in Ulster and Connacht, the provinces where the land was of poorer agricultural quality than in the other two Irish provinces.

Chapter seven

THE FAMINE

It was upon this tragic scene that the Famine was to descend. It was by any criterion the worst disaster that had overtaken any part of the British Isles since the Black Death in 1348. In a few short years a million people died of hunger: another million emigrated, many of them to die on the voyage to America or on arrival. The population of Ireland halved. This catastrophe had a permanent social effect on the character of the Irish people and a permanent political impact affecting not only the Irish in Ireland but even more the Irish communities that sprang up in the United States and in Australia, where bitter hatred of England is a continuing legacy. This terrible event that looms so naturally and so large in the minds of the Irish is almost totally forgotten in England, where the consequences of the Famine and its mishandling are resented, while the tragedy itself is forgotten. When I was a child in County Dublin walking along the roads near my home with our nurse and my young brother and sister in their pram, one was shut off from any view of the countryside by high stone walls. These had been put up by starving labourers in the 1840s as a means of providing work.

It is significant of the total unreality of Anglo-Irish relations at this period that in the months before the first onset of the potato blight, the House of Commons was stirred to its depths by the decision by Peel to raise the government grant to the Catholic seminary at Maynooth from £6,000 to £26,000 a year. One would have thought that in the prevailing state of the Irish peasantry this measure would pass almost unnoticed and further measures would have been passed to alleviate starvation. But this bill caused the Government of the day more trouble than any incident in the course of the Famine. Gladstone resigned from the Government on the issue and Peel only forced through the Bill with the aid of Opposition votes, while his position in his own party was irreparably damaged.

Since the potato crop was so essential to the very lives of a large proportion of the Irish public, one would have thought the closest watch would have been kept by the Government on its abundance or otherwise. But this was not so. There had been failures in the previous century and they grew more frequent, particularly in the 1830s. Any reduction in the potato crop meant starvation for some, as the ordinary peasant had no reserve, no margin on which to draw.

However, the blight that struck Ireland in 1845 was a new kind that came from North America and first declared itself in the Isle of Wight. In August, Dr Lindley, editor of the *Gardener's Chronicle* and founder of Kew Gardens, announced the destruction of the potato crop in Belgium and said, 'As for cure of this distemper there is none. We are visited by a great calamity.' Three weeks later he stopped the presses of his magazine to announce that the blight had reached Ireland and that the crops around Dublin were perishing. He asked, 'Where will Ireland be in the event of a universal potato rot?' The response of the British

Government to this calamitous news was what we have come to expect in our own day – a gush of optimistic blah. Peel wrote, 'There is such a tendency to exaggeration and inaccuracy in Irish reports that delay in acting on them is always desirable.'

The effect of the crop failure in 1845 was not as severe as it might have been – the crop before the blight struck was heavy and much of it had been dug before the disease arrived. But in 1846 the crop was a total failure; in 1847 not much better; 1848 was a bad year; in 1849 things were getting back to normal and in 1850 failure was only local and partial. The misery caused by the failure of their only source of food was aggravated by the fact that starving people ate the seed potatoes and that in any case potatoes in store were susceptible to the disease and rotted away.

When Peel realized that the failure of the potato crop was a serious calamity he put it to his colleagues that food would have to be imported and that this would logically involve the repeal of the Corn Laws. His party was the protectionist party and though Peel himself had been moving towards this decision for some years, it was one that caused violent feelings in his party. Part of the callous attitude in England to the Irish famine was caused by the ferocious political controversy that arose in England over the repeal of the Corn Laws. The occasion was the Irish Famine but the repeal did not benefit the Irish peasant and its long-term effect was to benefit the English industrial worker at the expense of the agricultural interest. It was the right decision under the circumstances, but it split the Conservative Party and won a torrent of abuse for Peel himself. The political effect was to distract attention from the Irish Famine and to concentrate it on events nearer home.

The major misconception of the British Government in dealing with the Famine was its touching faith in the virtue and in fact infallibility of market forces – *laissez-faire* as it was called. But over much of Ireland, particularly in the West, there were no market forces. There was a large population of peasants living on the potatoes they grew themselves. If the potatoes were uneatable, no market force could replace them. The peasant had no purchasing power at all. In order not to infringe the doctrine of *laissez-faire* Peel imported £100,000 worth of maize from America. As there was no existing trade in this grain, this was an ideologically acceptable move. But the amount was far too small, there were no facilities for its distribution and what do you do with the stuff when you get it? No wonder it was called 'Peel's Brimstone'. The Irish housewife had become accustomed to a diet of potatoes and had no idea how to cook anything else. Moreover in rural Ireland there were no mills where maize or any other grain could be ground nor any ovens where any kind of bread could be baked. This is the only defence that can be put forward for the fact that throughout the Famine large supplies of food were being exported from Ireland – often being conveyed to the ships that exported it by a strong armed guard. The oats and barley so exported with some wheat could have been used to relieve distress though any such effort would have encountered the difficulties of preparation and distribution mentioned above.

A prevalent idea in Government circles in London was that indeed the Government should do something about the starving Irish but that the main burden should fall on the landlords and richer members of the communities suffering from the Famine. In many areas there were no upper classes; the landlords in many cases were utterly callous; in others they were hopelessly insolvent. Such decisions could only be made by people at a distance with no knowledge of local conditions.

Of these the worst was Charles Edward Trevelyan, who was what we should consider the permanent head of the Treasury. He was a man of high intelligence and unbending rectitude, combining with these qualities all the worst characteristics of the Civil Service. Throughout the Famine he was the man in charge in London and was mainly concerned that public money was not wasted. To this admirable end all human feelings were sacrificed – a process made easier by the fact that in all the years of the famine he never went nearer the disaster areas than Dublin and he only once got as far as that. His letters to the men on the spot were a source of utter despair, since he refused to believe what he was told and gave instructions for the handling of millions of starving peasants that had no relation to reality. It is interesting that in spite of his total failure at the time of the Famine he suffered no loss of face and ended his career as Governor of Madras and Finance Minister of the Indian Government, while his son became Chief Secretary for Ireland. He seems to have been the type of Englishman who drives Irishmen to despair – a stickler for protocol with no discernible human feelings. In Ireland much is forgiven a man with a warm heart while the cold administrator brings out the Irishman's worst characteristics.

Owing to the Famine, the Irish peasants had nothing to sell, so no rent was paid. This led many landlords to evict their tenants and turn the land over to sheep or cattle. This was done in the most callous fashion – starving families being thrown into the road while troops and police pulled down their wretched cabins behind them. This naturally led to disorder and it was over a Coercion Bill for Ireland that Peel's Government was defeated. In spite of the defection of half his party over the Corn Laws he had a majority with the votes of the Opposition. But literally the moment the Repeal Bill passed the House of Lords, the Commons threw out the Coercion Bill and brought the Government down. The defeat had nothing to do with the Coercion Bill itself, in which the House showed little interest, but it was the means by which the Protectionist Tories could get their revenge.

With the departure of Peel from 10 Downing Street Lord John Russell came to office as Prime Minister. Trevelyan remained in charge of the Irish Famine but now he had Sir Charles Wood, grandfather of the Lord Halifax prominent in the politics of the 'thirties, as his Chancellor of the Exchequer. While Trevelyan's relations with Peel were not too cordial, he and Wood got on very well, and seem to have taken the same light-hearted view of the tragedy that was unfolding in Ireland.

Trevelyan and his Minister were anxious primarily that the Irish peasant should not become a permanent burden on the British exchequer, so in spite of frenzied protests from men on the spot orders were given in July 1846 that public works were to be abruptly terminated and depots for the distribution of free food were to be closed. It was assumed that the new potato

63

crop would be disease-free, but even if this had been true – and it was not – it would have been September or later before any worthwhile potatoes could be dug.

In fact, in early August the disease struck again. In 1845 the potato failure had been patchy and the grain harvest had been good. In 1846 the potato failure was total and the grain harvest very poor – and this was true of all Europe. Trevelyan was convinced that any relief that might be necessary should be provided by the local landlords and that supplies of food should be provided by the normal commercial channels. No food was to be bought by the Government: exports of grain from Ireland were to continue. He seems to have doubted whether the Irish were starving and *Punch* published a series of cartoons suggesting that any money subscribed for Irish relief would be devoted to the purchase of weapons. But the potato crop had failed; over large areas of the west of Ireland there was no food and no money to buy food; the distress was such that the Irish landlords could not possibly cope; the normal commercial channels in which Trevelyan and his ministers believed did not exist over the western half of Ireland. By September even Trevelyan was convinced that something must be done and he gave orders that maize was to be bought in North America, but by that time any available grain had been bought by the hungry Continental countries and the government's broker succeeded in acquiring only derisory amounts.

Difficulties arose over the nature of public works to be undertaken once the government thought of restarting them. Ireland needed drainage above all else to turn boggy fields into good farm-land, but drains would benefit some landowners more than others and so were out. The only acceptable form of public works were roads, and owing to previous famines the road system by this time was fully adequate. Indeed the County of Limerick was said to be 'regularly riddled with roads'.

After October in a bad year conditions tended to get worse and 1846 was no exception. Such food as was available was offered at exorbitant prices. Trevelyan found high prices very welcome as they would tend to bring out additional supplies of food to earn big profits. The government must not distribute food, as this would undercut the regular provision dealers and do them an injustice. Such doctrinaire nonsense would have been impossible had Trevelyan, Wood or any responsible minister travelled to the west of Ireland to see on the spot what was going on. But no such visit was paid.

Optimism about supplies from America was widespread in Westminster – ample supplies would be forthcoming in December and January. In Whitehall it was not realized that grain ships did not cross the North Atlantic in mid-winter. It was too dangerous and in any case all available grain had been shipped. In October information arrived that the Prussian government had bought all the rye, the French government all the wheat, there was no barley and the orders for maize were ten times the supply – and in any case all these were facts about the grain available for shipment in the spring of 1847. The difficulty of milling maize continued, but now the starving Irish were urged to eat the grain whole after boiling it for $1\frac{1}{2}$ hours. This was indigestible and caused acute intestinal pains and even serious internal damage.

In some cases the fear of disorder was greater than any interest in the Famine. Starving peasants saw well-fed soldiers arrive when all they wanted was food. A new argument was produced by Trevelyan as this ghastly winter drew on. To send food from England to Ireland would merely transfer hunger from one country to the other – so the Irish must just sweat it out.

Trevelyan and his minister Sir Charles Wood must have been unusually heartless people, but the composition of the Cabinet has to be borne in mind. Cabinets were smaller in those days, but three members, Lords Palmerston, Lansdowne and Clanricarde were Irish landlords, while Lord Cottenham was interested in mortgages on Irish property and the Prime Minister was promised a valuable Irish estate by his brother, the Duke of Bedford. So the interests of the Irish landlord was of paramount interest to an important minority of the British government.

I quote Mrs Woodham-Smith:

Autumn was now passing into winter. The nettles and blackberries, the edible roots and cabbage leaves on which hundreds of people had been eking out an existence disappeared: flocks of wretched beings, resembling human scare-crows, had combed the blighted potato fields over and over again until not a fragment of a potato that was conceivably edible remained.

Children began to die. In Skibbereen workhouse more than 50% of the children admitted after October 1st, 1846, died.

And now to add to the sufferings of the Irish people

the winter of 1846–7 proved to be the most severe in
living memory. It was not only the coldest but the
longest, with snow as early as November.

In December a Captain Wynne wrote to Trevelyan
from Clare Abbey:

'I ventured through the parish this day to ascertain the condition of the inhabitants, and, altho'
a man not easily moved, I confess myself unman-
ned by the intensity and extent of the suffering I
witnessed, more especially among the women and
little children, crowds of whom were to be seen
scattered over the turnip fields like a flock of
famishing crows, devouring the raw turnips,
mothers half naked, shivering in the snow and
sleet, uttering exclamations of despair while their
children were screaming with hunger. I am a
match for anything else I may meet with here,
but this I cannot stand.' (*The Great Hunger.*)

In the same month a Mr Cummins wrote a letter to
the Duke of Wellington, which was also published in
The Times. He had been to Skibbereen in County
Cork.

'I was surprised to find the wretched hamlet
apparently deserted. I entered some of the hovels
to ascertain the cause and the scenes which presented themselves were such as no tongue or pen can
convey the slightest idea of. In the first, six
famished and ghastly skeletons, to all appearances
dead, were huddled in a corner on some filthy
straw, their sole covering what seemed a ragged
horse-cloth, their wretched legs hanging about,

naked above the knees. I approached with horror and found by a low moaning they were alive – they were in a fever, four children, a woman and what had once been a man.' (*The Great Hunger.*)

And similar stories – or worse – poured in from all over the west of Ireland. In Skibbereen again at that time three corpses were found in the street, 197 died in a month in the workhouse and nearly 100 others had been found dead in their cabins or in the barns around. The landlords of Skibbereen, who were said to draw £50,000 a year from the district, do not seem to have bothered. Some landlords saw in the universal distress an opportunity to clear their estates of tenants with a view to more profitable grazing.

With the passage of time the government expenditure on public works increased to a very substantial figure, though the work was very badly organized. In February private enterprise began to function and maize started to arrive in substantial quantities in Cork and Limerick, but this was too late – destitution and disorganization had gone too far.

And then on top of famine came fever – typhus and relapsing fever that carried off huge numbers of people weakened by hunger. To the fever was added dysentery, known in the past as the 'bloody flux'. The British Government, running true to form, refused to believe at first the reports of a serious fever epidemic, but by the end of April 1847 did pass the necessary Irish Fever Bill. An aspect of the fever was that it was rife in Dublin, which had avoided the worst of the Famine. The diseases being infectious, and their cause unknown, it was unfortunately true that the death rate of patients in hospitals was higher than for those who remained at home. For reasons which are not clear the death rate from fever was higher among the upper classes than among the peasantry – this though they had not suffered from the Famine and were unlikely to use the overcrowded hospitals.

It was in the early months of 1847 that emigration became a serious factor in the situation. In the past, emigration had been more acceptable to the Presbyterians of Ulster than to the Catholics of the South, who were exceedingly reluctant to leave their country. Most of this emigration became attached to the timber trade – emigrants on the westward voyage, timber on the homeward one. The American government of the day was not particularly welcoming and initially most emigrants went to Canada, and in the summer months. The Catholic Irish did not willingly stay in Canada, which was of course at that time a British Colony, but moved as soon as possible into the United States. In the early months of the Famine emigration had increased, but only among the somewhat better-off members of the Catholic population.

With the spring of 1847 the combination of starvation and fever produced a very understandable panic and all who were able sought to leave the country. 30,000 reached the United States by sea because the St Laurence was still frozen, and the American government brought in restrictive legislation, protesting that they had no wish to become the poorhouse of Europe. Needless to say these wretched emigrants were braving the North Atlantic at the end of winter in vessels which in many cases were rightly called coffin ships. Even when the ship did arrive safely at its destination the

deaths from fever on the voyage were appalling –
one ship is recorded as losing 158 out of 476 and
another 108 out of 440. In many cases the emigration
was paid for by landlords who found it cheaper to ship
starving tenants to Canada than to keep them in the
workhouse. Lord Palmerston, afterwards Prime Minister, was particularly severely blamed in this regard.
Though his Sligo estates were well run, the thousands
of tenants he, or perhaps his agent, shipped out to
Canada arrived destitute and all but naked at the onset
of the Canadian winter. There are memorials in Mon-
treal to the 6,000 immigrants who died of fever and
were buried near the present Victoria Bridge, and on
Grosse Isle, where the immigrants landed in the first
place, the memorial records the burial of 5,294 persons
who, 'flying from pestilence and famine in Ireland in
the year 1847 found in America but a grave'.

In this terrible story there is not much to look back
on with satisfaction, but in Ireland the group that
comes through with most credit are the Quakers, and in
America, as soon as it was realized what was happening
and what was needed, the Americans were outstand-
ingly generous in the money they provided for food
and for shipping. The immigrants that reached the
United States by sea mostly landed in New York and
Boston, and even then their troubles were far from
over. The mortality rate among the poor Irish was
appalling – particularly among the children. Though
the German immigrants went inland, the Irish
remained in the slums of the big cities. The reason is
well given in a quotation from Mrs Woodham-Smith's
book:

A successful Irish farmer in Missouri who had worked in Ireland for sixpence a day now rejoiced in land and stock, no rent, light taxes, whiskey without government inspection, free shooting and, above all, social equality: yet he looked back regretfully to the days in Ireland where, after work, 'I could then go to a fair, a wake or a dance or I would spend the winter nights in a neighbour's house, cracking jokes by the turf fire. If I had there but a sore head I would have a neighbour within every hundred yards of me that would run to see me. But here everyone can get so much land, that they calls them neighbours that lives two or three miles off. And then I would sit down and cry, and curse him who made me leave home.'

And there is much of the Irish character summed up in those few lines. Above all, the Irishman needs his kind to talk and joke with.

Though the trans-Atlantic migration was the one that has received the publicity and has had the most damaging political effect on England, the larger emigration was to Great Britain. From 1846 the more heartless landlords had found a new means of removing starving peasants from their land. Instead of applying for eviction, they applied for a judgment against the tenant behind-hand with his rent. The tenant was then sent to prison and his family were left to fend for themselves. This method combined eviction with the break-up of the family and struck terror into the hearts of any family concerned. If they knew an application for judgment had been made, they fled. Their goal was inevitably the nearest port, and the cheapest voyage – sometimes free – was to Great Britain. It is the descendants of these fugitives that make up the large Irish minorities in Glasgow, Liverpool, Cardiff and elsewhere. Later emigration has tended to be to our inland towns and, with the exception of small pockets of traditional Catholics in Scotland and Lancashire, Irish immigrants are the ancestors of the large Catholic minority in Great Britain today. At least when the Irish reached an English or Scottish port they would not be allowed to die of hunger. Housing in the slums of Liverpool was appalling, but even so conditions were to be preferred to those in the west of Ireland at that time. The numbers were very large. By June 1847, 300,000 pauper Irish had landed in Liverpool in five months. Many of these moved on to North America, as Liverpool was the principal port of departure, but the majority stayed in Great Britain.

As 1847 wore on, the 700,000 or more labourers on public works were paid off and the soup kitchens closed down. Fine weather had come with the spring and Trevelyan looked back on a difficult corner successfully negotiated. In fact, of course, though the weather was better there had been few seed potatoes left, so the potato crop, when it came, would be quite inadequate and the attempt to push all relief measures off on to the Irish landlords was made without any regard for conditions on the spot. A large proportion of the landed estates were heavily encumbered and the landlords insolvent. Moreover, those who were capable of providing some relief were often more concerned with using every device to drive their tenants from their property so that it could be put to more profitable use. It is appalling to read of the utter lack of realism in the Parliamentary debates of the period and of the way the social life in the big houses in the eastern part of Ireland, notably in Dublin, continued as if starvation and fever were being experienced on a huge scale on some other planet.

By the summer of 1847 things looked somewhat better, the crops all over Europe looked promising and the Government was coming round to the view that more should be done of a permanent kind for Ireland – less relief and more new drainage schemes, harbours, railways and that kind of permanent improvement. Unfortunately at that moment a severe financial crisis broke out in London, with many bank failures, the collapse of commodity prices and a shortage of revenue. Sir Charles Wood declared he had no money for the Irish and had the effrontery to write of 'the safe and comfortable existence our rations have afforded them' and declared, 'They have hardly been decent while they have had their bellies full of our corn and their pockets of our money.'

This attitude on the part of the Chancellor of the Exchequer explains the continued efforts of the British Government to throw the full responsibility for the relief of the destitute and starving on to local resources. But in many places there were no local resources – in some the landlords were themselves hopelessly insolvent. In others there were no landlords – only starving peasants. Apart from the financial aspect of relief, there was the administrative. The Board of Guardians in many parts of the West was expected to cope with distribution over an impossibly large area. Mrs Woodham-Smith quotes the Union of Ballina in County

Mayo, which covered over half a million acres and contained over 120,000 people. A Quaker of the day said of this Union that in English terms it stretched from London to Buckingham and Oxford in one direction and from London to Basingstoke in another, with the poorhouse at St Albans. Moreover it included Erris, a vast tract of desolate country bordering on the Atlantic, where distress 'wore its most appalling form'.

Nevertheless Trevelyan and his minister pressed on with the attempt to shift on to Irish shoulders the burden of relief. While no doubt there were areas where this could be done, there were areas in the West where this was impossible and where the attitude of some landlords was not to pay rates to the Poor Law Guardians but to evict their tenants even in this period of terrible distress. Lord John Russell had been a liberal-minded minister in his earlier career but at this time all he had to say was, 'The state of Ireland for the next few months must be one of great suffering. Unhappily the agitation for Repeal [i.e. Home Rule] has contrived to destroy nearly all sympathy in this country.'

In the winter of 1847 conditions returned to where they had been the previous year. Though the crops were good, where planted, the utter destitution of the population meant that the crops were far too small to feed the people, and officials in London believed, or pretended to believe, that conditions were not nearly so bad as they were made out to be by reports from the officials on the spot. It is not surprising that under the conditions then existing there began the agrarian outrages that were to be a feature of Irish history in later decades. In the autumn and winter of 1847 seven

74

landlords were shot, six of them being killed. In the same period ten others, occupiers of land though not landlords, were murdered.

Mrs Woodham-Smith sums up the position in Ireland at the end of 1847:

> So with 15,000 extra troops in the country, a campaign of terrorisation being waged, workhouses enlarged to take 150,000 additional inmates and, in the distressed unions, people dying of starvation both inside the workhouses and outside them, with rates impossible to collect, employment nonexistent, fever still raging and the people pauperised and wretched as never before, Ireland passed from 1847 into 1848.

Though fears of rebellion were expressed by Lord Clarendon, the Viceroy, in fact these murders were no part of a concerted effort, but were born of despair and a lust for revenge. The political effects of the Famine were brought out by one Fintan Lalor. He is described as a poor, distorted, ill-favoured, hunchbacked creature of about forty years of age. He had lived in total obscurity on a farm in Queen's County, but in January 1847 wrote a long and remarkable letter to *The Nation,* the nationalist paper of the day. His theme was that 'The future of Ireland lay in possession of the land: forever henceforth the owners of our soil must be Irish and the importance of the famine was that it opened the way for an agrarian revolution.' The Young Ireland movement, which had been founded in 1842 as an offshot of O'Connell's Repeal Association, was composed of younger and more extreme members than was its parent body. But Lalor's call to action went further, as he was prepared, as Young Ireland were not, to contemplate armed insurrection. However, this attitude changed in 1848, the year of revolution all over Europe, when the French in February rose and forced Louis-Philippe to abdicate. In succeeding months there was much wild talk of armed rebellion, particularly in John Mitchel's paper, the *United Irishman*. But wild and bloodthirsty words were backed by no organization and though the words frightened the British government the conspirators achieved nothing. Instructed by the Pope, the Catholic priesthood played no part in this agitation, as they had in previous ones. After much marching and speech-making the rising ended in a scuffle at the Widow McCormack's cabbage patch. The Irish were too hungry to fight. However, more serious than this abortive rising was the second total failure of the potato crop. In 1847 there had been little or no blight: the trouble had been the lack of seed potatoes and in consequence the inadequate crop. In 1848 the seed potatoes were mostly available but the blight struck again. By the terms of the law under which rates were levied, landlords had to evict their tenants in many cases as the only way to avoid their own ruin. In other cases the landlord was bankrupt but unable to sell his property owing to the slow and complicated legal procedure. The land had then no effective owner and the tenants suffered.

Sir William Butler described an eviction and a 'tumbling' which he witnessed as a boy in Tipperary.

The sheriff, a strong force of police, and above all

the crowbar brigade, a body composed of the lowest and most debauched ruffians, were present. At a signal from the sheriff the work began. The miserable inmates of the cabins were dragged out upon the road: the thatched roofs were torn down and the earthen walls battered in by crowbars: the screaming women, the half-naked children, the paralysed grandmother and the tottering grandfather were hauled out. It was a sight I have never forgotten. I was 12 years old at the time, but I think if a loaded gun had been put into my hands I would have fired into that crowd of villains as they plied their horrible trade. ... The winter of 1848–49 dwells in my memory as one long night of sorrow. (*The Great Hunger.*)

The natural result of this fresh calamity was a fresh wave of emigration. But the Canadians had introduced measures to prevent thousands of destitute paupers being dumped on their shores. So the emigrants were not the **panic**-stricken peasants of earlier years but farmers of some substance able to pay for their passage to North America.

Owing to efforts at rebellion in the early months of 1848 the government in England was even less sympathetic to Irish needs that it had been before. Trevelyan would have liked to abolish outdoor relief altogether, and in spite of the potato crop failure got the figure down to £200,000 in October, though it rose again to £400,000 in December. The effect of government parsimony was not only felt by the peasants at the bottom of the social pyramid but all the way up – more landlords were ruined, shop-keepers even in prosperous towns were bankrupt. A Poor Law inspector spoke of 'the dread of the break-up of all society'. Yet Lord John Russell wrote:

We have subscribed, worked, visited, clothed for the Irish, millions of money, years of debate, etc. etc. The only return is rebellion and calumny. Let us not grant, lend, clothe, etc. any more and see what that will do.' Benjamin Jowett, the famous Master of Balliol, said, 'I have always felt a certain horror of political economists since I heard one of them say that he feared the famine of 1848 in Ireland would not kill more than a million people, and that would scarcely be enough to do much good.'

In 1849 Thomas Carlyle paid a visit to Ireland. This is part of his account of the town of Kildare, in the most prosperous part of Ireland: 'A wretched wild village, like a village in Dahomey: beggars, beggars, wretched streets: the extremity of raggedness.' Even *The Times,* which had opposed help for Ireland, felt something should be done. Trevelyan, however, had learnt nothing in the previous years and returned to his insistence that any relief for the destitute in Ireland must be paid for by the Irish. The idea was a rate-in-aid to be paid by the more prosperous areas for the relief of those that were bankrupt. In all, over £300,000 was to be raised in this way. But before the Act could be carried into effect a further calamity befell Ireland – a cholera epidemic.

Lord Clarendon, the Viceroy, wrote to Lord John Russell, the Prime Minister, about the resignation of a

Mr Twisleton, the official responsible for relief measures in Ireland. 'He thinks that the destitution here is so horrible, and the indifference of the House of Commons to be so manifest, that he is an unfit agent of a policy which must be one of extermination.'

Not only were government measures even more reluctant than before, but private charity dried up and the Quakers closed down their splendid relief work.

It was at this unlikely moment that it was decided that the Queen should visit Ireland. The idea was that her visit would provide a stimulus to trade. On any view the decision was a remarkable one, though it has to be remembered that at that time, as earlier, the nationalist aspiration was for a self-governing Ireland sharing its monarch with Great Britain. In fact at a meeting of the Young Ireland party in 1848 the Queen's health had been drunk in tea, while *God Save the Queen* was played on an Irish harp.

The *Freeman's Journal* recommended that one visit to a hut in Connaught, one view of a 'cleared' estate in the south, a pencil sketch showing an unroofed cabin with the miserable emaciated inhabitants cast out and perishing on the dung-heap beside it, would be a better portrait of Ireland than the beauties of Killarney. In fact the Queen only visited Cork and Dublin. In both places she had a rapturous reception deeply moving to all beholders. She returned to Ireland on three subsequent occasions but the warm reception was not repeated. Though the Queen's visit enjoyed the greatest possible success, it was a purely personal one and had no political consequences of any kind.

Though the Famine was now officially over, there

were still one million destitute persons in the work-houses and on relief, and the philanthropist Sidney Godolphin Osborne, travelling in the west of Ireland in 1849, frequently 'saw dead bodies lying by the side of the road'.

Emigration to North America and to Australia continued on a very large scale, averaging 200,000 a year from 1848 to 1852. To this has to be added the emigration to Great Britain.

The means were brutal but the social effects of the Famine had some favourable results. The over-population of the west of Ireland was reduced to more manageable proportions: the intense sub-division of small farms was reversed and numbers of encumbered estates were sold up and new landowners, many of them Catholics, installed in their stead. But dependence on the potato continued, the precarious tenure of the peasants was unaltered: nothing was done by government or landlords to improve and bring up to date the farming methods of the Irish peasant. The relief given by the British government to the starving Irish had been grudging and wholly inadequate, while the effect on British public opinion of Ireland's distress was merely irritation and even anger. No Cabinet Minister went to the west of Ireland to see what conditions were like, though for their holidays they journeyed to the south of France and to Italy. When on pleasure bent, distance was no obstacle.

The original emigrants who founded what after-wards became the United States went away in a spirit of economic or religious enterprise. It was a quest for greater freedom. In the case of the Irish emigration at the time of the Famine and immediately after, it was a flight in panic from a land that seemed to be cursed. As the century drew on the causes of emigration changed. There was of course the lure of those who had made good in the United States writing home to invite their relations to join them. But the main motive behind emigration from the 'fifties of the last century to the present day has been the change in the social conditions of rural Ireland. Until the Famine, land was divided and subdivided into ever-smaller plots of ground, and early marriage was the custom. After the Famine, land was consolidated into larger units which were passed on by the farmer to his heir, who tended to marry in middle age. The farmer would hope to accumulate the dowry for a daughter who would marry a farmer in the neighbourhood. For any other sons or daughters there was no place except as unpaid servants. Movement into the towns, to England or overseas emigration was the only alternative to lifelong servitude and celibacy. Here, too, emigration was more or less compulsory – it was not an adventure. The emigrant did not see himself as a pioneer seeking a better life. In any case an Irishman has a passionate attachment to his beautiful country and to a way of life that only seems possible within its borders.

Chapter eight

GLADSTONE, PARNELL AND HOME RULE

In 1850 there were to be two elements in Irish Nationalist politics. One was the continuing tradition from
the rebellion of 1798 to Emmet and Young Ireland, a
tradition that included a demand for an independent
republic and in Lalor's case emphasized the need for
agrarian reform. The second was the formation of an
Irish party at Westminster. From 1800 to 1850, though
there were 100 Irish M.P.s, eventually 103 in spite of
the fall in the population, they had shown very little
differentiation from their British fellows. The formation
of a group of Irish M.P.s specifically interested in Irish
affairs arose improbably from the decision by the Pope
to restore the English hierarchy. It caused an immense
hoo-ha in England and led to the passing of the Ecclesiastical Titles Act under which the Catholic Church may
not have bishops with the same titles as Anglican ones.

Though the rising of 1848 was a paltry affair, one of
the consequences of this episode was the emergence
of James Stephens, who escaped to Paris where he
met other European revolutionary groups. In 1856 he
returned to Ireland to spy out the land and on St
Patrick's Day 1858 he founded a new secret society
'to make Ireland an independent democratic republic'.
This in time developed into the Fenian movement and
the Irish Republican Brotherhood – the I.R.B., which
is regarded by the present members of the I.R.A. as

82

their forebear. While the conspirators used Paris as their base, money was to come, then as now, from the United States and mainly from New York, where the population at that time was one-quarter Irish. The American end was looked after by John O'Mahony, who seems to have been a good organizer – and organization was not otherwise the conspirators' strong suit. Stephens started a newspaper in Dublin, the *Irish People,* which, however, was taken over by O'Donovan Rossa, another big name in the conspiratorial politics of that period.

Fenianism ran into strong opposition from the Catholic Church. This was partly due to Catholic condemnation of all secret societies and partly due to the trend of politics on the Continent and particularly in Italy where the Pope was to lose his temporal power over the States of the Church. This opposition was carried to great lengths by Cardinal Cullen, Archbishop of Armagh and subsequently of Dublin, but to even greater lengths by Dr Moriarty, Bishop of Kerry, who brought down on the Fenian leaders 'God's heaviest curse, his withering, blasting, blighting curse', adding that for their punishment 'eternity is not long enough, nor Hell hot enough'. At least these Irishmen said what they thought and in unambiguous language.

While money was being raised in America and Irish soldiers were being sworn in as Fenians, Stephens promised that 1866 would be the great year of the final uprising. In fact little happened except the invasion of Canada by a small armed group from the United States. This was to have created an international crisis and, with luck, war between England and the United States. This little group were of course rounded up, as the Fenian Society had been infiltrated by informers, a common feature of Irish societies in later years. In spite of the total failure of this Canadian venture it was renewed with equal lack of success on two further occasions. At this point the influence of veterans of the American Civil War became important. These were men who had experience of war and believed more in fighting than in speech-making. A number of them became interested in Irish affairs and it is their influence that led to the disastrous uprising of 1867. It was badly organized, inadequately armed and had the bad luck to be launched in a snow-storm – and snow-storms are not frequent in Ireland. The principal centres were in Dublin and Cork, but the insurgents had no success whatever. The leaders were rounded up and sentenced to long terms in prison, though death sentences were commuted. The lasting importance of this rising was that an attempt was made in Manchester to release two important conspirators from a prison van. The prisoners were released, but in blowing off the lock of the van a policeman was accidentally killed. Subsequently three men were tried for murder and after an unsatisfactory trial were condemned and executed. These men became known as the Manchester martyrs, and were important names in the Nationalist tradition. Later in the year an attempt was made to release Irish prisoners from Clerkenwell gaol by blowing up a wall of the prison. Unfortunately a number of quite innocent people were killed, thus reinforcing the view of the militants in the English establishment that what was needed was even firmer and more repressive government.

In the short term the events of 1866–7 were of no

importance, but in the long term they had three effects: firstly, to supply a link between 1798 and independence in 1922 – a vital link for the Nationalists; secondly, for the first time in Irish affairs the American link became important; and thirdly, it convinced Mr Gladstone that something serious must be done about Ireland. Before the Famine, Gladstone had written, in a letter to his wife, 'Ireland, Ireland, that cloud in the west, that coming storm, the minister of God's retribution upon cruel and inveterate and but half-atoned injustice!' In the intervening years he played no useful part in Irish affairs, but that was not to remain true after 1867.

In 1868 he became Prime Minister and set about some Irish reforms. He attempted three and succeeded with one-and-a-half. His success was the disestablishment of the Anglican Church in Ireland: his failure was the attempt to set up an un-denominational – in practice, a Catholic – university. His Irish Land Bill, designed to protect the status of the tenant, was not nearly as effective as he had hoped. And of course even if all three measures had been triumphant successes, only the third would have had any serious effect on the nationalist pressure.

At this stage the nationalist cause was taken up by Isaac Butt, son of a Protestant clergyman in Donegal and for long an M.P. Before he succumbed to the bottle he had launched in 1870 what became the first beginnings of the Home Rule movement. The body he sought to set up was the Home Government Association, which was to press for a separate government for Ireland which would be responsible for all Ireland's domestic affairs. It has to be remembered that there were always two reasons for Repeal, or Home Rule as it was afterwards called. The first was resentment over rule by aliens and the second, perhaps more important in the earlier years, was the incompetence of the British Government in Ireland. Disraeli in 1844 said it was the weakest executive in the world, and he was not far wrong.

In 1874 there was a General Election, the first after the adoption of the Secret Ballot. Fifty-nine Irish members were returned, pledged with varying degrees of enthusiasm to Home Rule. They were not a homogeneous body and anyway Butt was thinking in terms of an Imperial Federation of which Ireland would be one of the federated bodies. He was a man of great charm and sought to gain his ends by goodwill and co-operation.

One of the new Irish members was J. G. Biggar, who sounds an unattractive type, but formed the correct assessment of the mentality of the government and House of Commons of his day. Much more was to be gained by obstruction than by co-operation. As a convert to Catholicism and as a businessman who addressed a House of Commons of a far more aristocratic character than it has today with a harsh Belfast accent, he must have been accustomed to unpopularity both in London and at home. But unpopularity acted as no deterrent. He also realized first among the Irish members at Westminster that only rigid discipline could make them a force to be reckoned with and it is in fact from the Irish example of those days that sprang the rigid discipline by the Whips of M.P.s in the House today.

Biggar's manner, appearance and background were

such that he could not hope to become the leader of the Irish Nationalist group in the House of Commons. But in 1875 a by-election in Meath brought to the House Charles Stewart Parnell. Most unpredictably he proved to be the leader for whom the Irish Nationalists were looking. As a Protestant and a landlord, educated in England, he hardly seemed to have the makings of a Nationalist. At his first entry into politics he was almost tongue-tied but in time developed into a good speaker who imposed his views on his audience by his passionate convictions, his commanding appearance and his extreme self-confidence. Though his father, Sir John Parnell, was very much a member of the Ascendancy, his mother was an American, daughter of an admiral who fought against the British in the war of 1812. She was strongly anti-British and communicated her feelings to her children.

Parnell's appearance in 1875 was followed in 1878 by that of another leading figure in Irish politics, John Dillon. It was mainly Dillon who drove Butt from the leadership of the group shortly before his death. Other figures to emerge into prominence at this time were John Devoy and Michael Davitt. The former operated in America where the Clan-na-Gael was of growing importance in Irish politics: the latter was born in County Mayo but, when his family were evicted, emigrated to Lancashire, where he lost an arm in a mill accident. The problem facing the nationalists was the divergence between the Parliamentarians led by Parnell and the revolutionaries in the Irish Republican Brotherhood. Biggar, who had been a member of the latter, was even expelled because of his parliamentary activities. Eventually they were to come together in

the 'New Departure'. There was a good deal of misunderstanding over secret agreements secretly arrived
at, but the result was that the parliamentarians and
the revolutionaries continued to pursue a common
purpose – Irish Independence –on two different levels.

At this point a new factor emerged – or rather an
old factor re-asserted itself. Depression in agricultural
prices, partly owing to competition from America,
hit both Great Britain and Ireland. Simultaneously
the potato crop failed. So the miserably poor farmers
of the west of Ireland lost not only their income from
seasonal work in England but their subsistence in Ireland as well. The result was starvation as it had not
been seen for thirty years. General Charles Gordon,
killed later at Khartoum, wrote to Gladstone at the end
of 1880:

> I must say from my own observation that the
> state of our fellow countrymen in the west of
> Ireland is worse than that of any people in the
> world, let alone Europe. I believe that these
> people are made as we are, that they are patient
> beyond belief, loyal, but, at the same time, broken
> spirited and desperate, living on the verge of star-
> vation in places in which we would not keep our
> cattle. (*Ireland Since the Famine*.)

With the hardship consequent on the agricultural
depression in England and the potato failure, rents
were not – could not – be paid. Evictions followed
and outrages followed the evictions, culminating in
1880 when over 2,000 families were driven from their
homes, and the number of outrages and cattle-maim-

ing, burning and shooting also reached a record level of 2,500.

It was this development in the Irish countryside that led the nationalists back to Lalor's belief that the land problem was a central factor in Irish politics. The idea had previously been to give the Irish tenant security while now, increasingly, it was to give the farmer the ownership of his farm.

Part of the Land agitation was organized so that no one could take over a farm from which the tenants had been evicted. It was in pursuit of this policy that Lord Erne's agent, Captain Boycott, was ostracized, thus giving a new word to our own and other languages.

The election of 1880 brought Gladstone back into office. From an Irish point of view the feature of the election was the success of Parnell, who was returned for three constituencies and was subsequently elected Chairman of the Home Rule M.P.s. While his own success was on strictly constitutional lines, his support came in great measure from the Land League, which became the strongest political force in the Irish countryside.

While Gladstone was known to be generally sympathetic to the Irish, he was also very conscious that he was responsible for law and order. His introduction of Coercion Bills caused an uproar in Parliament. Parnell was urged to withdraw from Parliament with his followers and set up a sort of parliament in Dublin. However, he decided to continue his agitation at Westminster. His more militant colleagues would have landed Ireland in a civil war which, as Parnell could well see, would have inevitably led to a nationalist defeat. Moreover the government brought in a Land

Act to give tenants greater security of tenure. Though it was too complicated and by no means solved all the problems of landlord and tenant, it was a big step forward. Parnell could see this but also knew that it would by no means satisfy his more militant followers, so in effect he facilitated its passage while denouncing the measure in the most ferocious terms – to such an extent that he was arrested and imprisoned. While he was in jail agrarian outrages increased – mostly murders and attempted murders. In the spring of 1882 Parnell was released as a result of what was called the 'Kilmainham Treaty'. The government would amend the Land Act and Parnell would use his influence to stop the terrorism. Unfortunately the 'Treaty' was marred by the murder of Lord Frederick Cavendish and Mr T. H. Burke, the new Chief Secretary and his Under-Secretary, on their arrival in Dublin a few days later. The murderers belonged to a small secret society which seems to have had nothing to do with the main nationalist groups of that time.

The effect of the Land Act and the Treaty was to transfer the main interest of the nationalists from land reform to Home Rule and from mass pressure in the countryside to constitutional agitation. It is interesting that this shift in emphasis led to a steep decline in the very large financial contributions from America. However, though pinched for money, the Home Rulers in the 1885 election scored a huge success, winning every seat in Ireland except Trinity College, Dublin, and the constituencies in East Ulster. They even won one in Liverpool. The members returned to this parliament were more middle-class, more numerous and more disciplined than any previous Irish pressure group; moreover in Parnell they had a superb leader.

Joseph Chamberlain tried to persuade the Liberal government to set up a Central Board to have responsibility for education and communications in Ireland. He seems to have been under the quite false impression that this would have satisfied Parnell. But he could not get his Cabinet colleagues to agree and in any case a combination of Irish members and Conservatives shortly afterwards defeated the Liberals and Lord Salisbury took office. Parnell was interested in self-government for Ireland and was not particular how he got it. For his purpose Conservatives were as good as Liberals. The Conservatives passed another Land Act and appointed Lord Carnarvon, a sympathetic peer, as Lord Lieutenant with a seat in the Cabinet. In the ensuing election – the second in 1885 – Parnell did his best with the Irish vote in England to help the Conservatives, but the Liberals won 86 more seats than the Conservatives, exactly balancing Parnell's 86 followers. This was an unstable situation anyway, but Lord Salisbury seems to have decided to humour his Tories rather than the Irish and announced in the Queen's speech the introduction of yet another Coercion bill. The Liberals and Home Rulers combined on this issue to defeat the Conservatives, and Mr Gladstone returned to power.

Mr Gladstone was a devout Christian and had come to regard the Irish as a moral rather than a political problem. He had supported nationalism in the Balkans and Italy, how could he deny it to the Irish? To him the argument, very prevalent at the time, that the Irish were a backward people, quite unfitted for self-government, was wholly unconvincing. Mr Gladstone would have preferred Home Rule to have come about with a Conservative Government as they would have a much better chance of getting their measure through the House of Lords. However, the responsibility was now his. But while Gladstone was convinced on moral grounds that Home Rule was necessary, his government were by no means equally convinced. In particular Chamberlain, a most formidable political force, would have none of the idea and resigned. It was Parnell's opinion that it was his resignation that killed Home Rule. The motives for his resignation are not all that clear. He had been convinced – perhaps by O'Shea – that Parnell would agree to his idea of a Central Board. When Parnell rejected this, Chamberlain felt he had been double-crossed. Moreover when he went on a goodwill tour to Ireland his reception was so hostile that the tour had to be abandoned. So personal resentment may well have been an element in his opposition.

The Home Rule Bill of 1886 seems a very moderate measure to us now – for instance, foreign policy, defence, customs, trade and control of the currency were all reserved for the government in Westminster. However, when the bill was presented to the House of Commons it was rejected and Gladstone resigned. The defeat brought about two results. Hitherto Parnell had been able to play off Conservatives and Liberals against each other in his efforts to secure Home Rule. From 1886 the Liberals had adopted Home Rule and the Conservatives had rejected it. The second and more serious consequence was that in their efforts to secure the defeat of the bill Lord Randolph Churchill and Joseph Chamberlain had made use of the argument that there were two Irelands and that it would be unjust to hand over Irish Unionists to a native Irish government, for which they felt nothing but revulsion. They invented the slogan: 'Ulster will fight and Ulster will be right'. The slogan was followed up by drilling and the purchase of arms – the beginning of what we see in the Six Counties today.

As if Ireland had not suffered enough, at this date she was hit by yet another agricultural depression. Conditions had been fairly peaceful while the fate of the Home Rule Bill was in doubt, but once it had been rejected, trouble followed. Parnell was in ill health and was having trouble in his private life and so was not involved. But his more militant followers, Dillon, O'Brien and Harrington, launched 'The Plan of Campaign'. Under this plan the tenants on an estate were to offer the landlord lower rents all round, and if they were not accepted no rent would be paid. The money would be paid into an estate fund to help the tenants when they were evicted. If the estate fund proved inadequate, the National League was to be called in to help. This National League arose out of the earlier more revolutionary Land League but was under firm parliamentary control. It existed primarily to provide an electoral machine for Parnell and his party. Any new tenants who took over farms from which the tenants had been evicted were to be ostracized, as was everyone who helped them. The Plan remained in operation for some seven years or so and led to a certain amount of bitterness and disorder, particularly in the Counties of Tipperary, Limerick and Kerry. It was met by vigorous counter-measures by the Chief Secretary, A. J. Balfour, afterwards Prime Minister, known in Ireland as Bloody Balfour. Not only was his administration exceptionally ruthless in its attempt to maintain law and order, but he also enlisted the support of the Catholic hierarchy. Eventually the Pope condemned the Plan in a rescript in 1888. The Catholic bishops bowed to the Papal decision but lower down the Catholic community it was felt the Church had intervened in a purely political matter and one in which they appeared on the side of the rich against the poor.

In 1887 *The Times* published some letters purporting to have been written in 1882 which clearly implicated Parnell in the campaign of agrarian violence. The government set up a commission, widely believed to be partisan and anti-nationalist. In 1889 the main question was solved when Richard Pigott admitted under cross-examination that he had forged the letters. In these years Parnell was the most powerful political figure at Westminster and this vindication by an unfriendly commission boosted his prestige still further. The Plan of Campaign had never been his idea. He had sought to get Home Rule by constitutional means and regarded any degree of violence as irrelevant. If, in the end, constitutional advance was finally blocked, then, his argument ran, would be the time to consider extra-constitutional measures.

Although the Home Rule Bill of 1886 had been defeated in the Commons it was generally believed that Gladstone would soon be back in office and that the conditions were now more favourable for the passing of an acceptable bill.

It was at this moment that Yeats's Fourth Bell began to toll. It is a tangled and dramatic story, which I will not attempt to give in full. Parnell had a mistress, Kitty

O'Shea, wife of a Captain O'Shea, M.P. for Galway. In 1890 O'Shea brought a divorce action against his wife, citing Parnell. The case did not present Parnell in a heroic light – evidence in a divorce case seldom does. O'Shea got his divorce and Parnell married his Kitty. O'Shea contended in court that he had brought the case as soon as he learnt of his wife's association with Parnell. This seems to have been untrue. He had known about it for years, but held his hand since Kitty was hoping for a large legacy from an aunt who would not have left the money to Kitty if she had known about her domestic affairs. In fact O'Shea seems to have used the situation to blackmail Parnell into getting him an Irish seat in the House of Commons. What is so difficult to understand is that Parnell, with his passionate attachment to the Nationalist cause, should over a period of years have allowed it to be jeopardized by this affair. He must have known that its permanent concealment was unlikely and that if it hit the headlines he and his cause would suffer shipwreck. Perhaps he, as so many others since, had got away with so much that he had come to think of himself as invulnerable.

As a result of the divorce case, the Irish party was split and Gladstone let it be known that any co-operation between himself and Parnell was no longer possible. The Catholic hierarchy in Ireland took the same line. There have been accusations of hypocrisy over the attitudes of the various groups concerned. But what else could they do? Gladstone depended on a large non-conformist following which left him no other course. Parnell fought on for some months but he was ill and defeated and died not long after. It is likely that Gladstone knew of the Parnell–Kitty

O'Shea relationship and was prepared to look the other way as long as he could. The divorce case left him no option.

Nevertheless nearly ninety years later Parnell is still a great name in Irish history – he put Home Rule on the political map; his Irish Party was the first rigidly disciplined group in the House of Commons; the Land Act of 1881, for which he was largely responsible, led to the emancipation of the Irish tenant. Very few men achieved so much.

In the General Election of 1892 Gladstone had only a small majority by including the Irish Nationalists. I think it is William Gladstone's principal claim to political greatness that he saw, as we can now do, but as most of his contemporaries did not, that Ireland was the crucial issue facing the Nation. Failure to provide an answer would involve the break-up of the United Kingdom with repercussions throughout the British Empire. So, though an old man with a precarious majority, he introduced a Home Rule Bill which this time passed the House of Commons but was defeated in the House of Lords by an overwhelming majority. It is difficult to see why the Lords were so hostile. No doubt there were still some influential Irish landlords; their lordships are normally against innovations of any sort, and perhaps they were afraid that self-government in Ireland might lead to similar demands from other provinces or colonies. Whatever the answer, the Home Rule Bill was killed, Gladstone finally retired, and Home Rule receded into the political background.

After the Parnellite débâcle a ferocious struggle ensued for the leadership of the Irish party split between Parnellites and anti-Parnellites. In the end, nine years later, the party was re-united under John Redmond, who was one of the Parnellite faction. He led the party until the Easter Rising of 1916, when events had far overtaken him and his policy.

So far we have been talking about political developments in Ireland, but in the last decade of the century a new factor emerged. Up to this time it had been customary to represent the Irishman as a figure of fun. He was a low-grade human being – in the eyes of English propaganda – incapable of governing himself, resembling in some ways the many savage tribes to be found throughout our colonial empire.

However, a start was made in 1884 with the Gaelic Athletic Association to promote the playing of Irish football and Irish hockey. This was followed in 1892 by the National Literary Society and in 1893 by the far more important Gaelic League. The Gaelic League was founded by Douglas Hyde to revive an interest in Gaelic culture and the Irish language, which was still widely spoken in the west of Ireland. The Abbey Theatre, founded in 1897 by Lady Gregory and W. B. Yeats, became a cultural centre of more than Irish importance. It is not sufficiently realized in England that the great literary figures of the early years of this century were mostly Irish. Apart from Shaw, Yeats, Oscar Wilde and James Joyce, there was a host of lesser men – Synge and George Moore among many others. These men were all – or nearly all – Protestants, but very Irish. I mention this not to extol Protestantism but to emphasize the salient fact that Irish personality and Irish culture were essential features of their contribution. They were not just Englishmen brought up in Ireland. That Catholic Ireland's contribution to English literature came later is not to be wondered at considering the economic, social and political degradation to which she had been subjected for so long.

Though these were cultural movements and movements in which many of the participants played no political part, the revolutionaries were keenly interested. The Irish Republican Brotherhood and Arthur Griffith's 'Sinn Fein' were two of the revolutionary bodies concerned. They saw in these cultural developments an enhancement of their own nationalism.

The Conservatives returned to power in 1895 and remained in office until 1906, first under the Prime Ministership of Lord Salisbury and subsequently under that of his nephew A. J. Balfour. With the death of Parnell the Irish party at Westminster was deeply divided and the Conservative Party was unsympathetic to Home Rule in any form. But, though this was true on the Parliamentary level, Irish aspirations at the grass roots remained unaltered. By successive land acts of one kind and another Ireland was becoming a land of peasant proprietors, whose prosperity was strengthened by Horace Plunkett's success in establishing creameries on a co-operative basis. The outcome was that the landlord and tenant problem gradually faded away. The Conservative Government seems to have supposed that if specific grievances could be eliminated, the demand for Home Rule would disappear. The same misjudgment has re-asserted itself in 1973, when we see the government pouring money into Northern Ireland and eliminating grievances in local government under the impression that it can thus buy off the demand for a United Ireland. In any case any longstanding political agitation does not remain indefinitely at the same intensity but comes and goes in waves, giving complacent governments the chance at the trough of a wave to maintain that their measures are at last yielding results.

In 1898 came the centenary of the rebellion of 1798, which was celebrated with much oratory, if not much else. Then came the Boer War, which served to show the world that British military might was not all it appeared to be. Two Irish 'brigades' fought on the side of the Boers against the British Army, but this had no more than propaganda value.

Parliamentary ways of achieving Home Rule having collapsed, the younger men turned to other methods. In this they were encouraged by Arthur Griffith and his paper, *United Irishman*. Griffith was also a member of the Irish Republican Brotherhood, the secret society which had remained in being throughout the ups and downs of nineteenth-century Irish politics.

In 1905 Griffith summoned a National Council Convention which led in 1908 to a merger with the Sinn Fein League and the establishment of 'Sinn Fein'. The words mean 'ourselves' and the policy was set down as 'the re-establishment of the independence of Ireland'. At the same time the title of Griffith's paper was changed from *United Irishman* to *Sinn Fein*. In 1907 the veteran Fenian Tom Clarke returned to Ireland from the United States and from then on the I.R.B. became increasingly active, even publishing a paper called *Irish Freedom* in 1910.

While events in Ireland were pursuing a more or less revolutionary course, in England the situation changed dramatically with the landslide defeat of the Conservatives in 1906. The new Prime Minister, Sir Henry Campbell-Bannerman, was sympathetic to Irish aspirations and his party was committed in principle to Home Rule. Campbell-Bannerman has not had his due in histories of the period, and anyway he died in office after only two years. His sympathy with Ireland was real and was typical of the man who had invited violent abuse during the Boer War by denouncing the camps into which Boer women and children were herded and in which so many died.

The problem in getting any Home Rule Bill passed into law was that such a bill passed by the Liberal Party in the House of Commons was bound to be thrown out in the House of Lords. But following the Budget crisis of 1909 and two subsequent General Elections, the Lords' power of absolute veto was removed and Home Rule at once became a serious item on the parliamentary calendar – particularly as the Irish members held the balance of power in the House of Commons.

That Home Rule was becoming a practical possibility had not escaped the notice of the Conservatives and in particular of Sir Edward Carson. The failure of Balfour at the General Election of 1906 led to his retirement in 1911 and replacement by Bonar Law, a colourless Canadian of Northern Irish ancestry who was ready to let Carson make Ulster the rallying cry of the Conservatives when the conservation of the veto of the House of Lords seemed no longer possible.

While Carson was occupied with organizing Ulster in its resistance to Home Rule, and while the Parliamentary drama in Westminster was continuing on its way with the Home Rule Bill starting its progress over the delaying veto of the House of Lords, Dublin was being convulsed with strikes. These were organized by James Larkin, mainly in the docks and transport industries, ably abetted by James Connolly, who was to become the leading figure in Irish Socialist history. The strikes were fought on the employers' side by William Martin Murphy, a leading Irish employer, proprietor of the *Irish Independent* and much else. Larkin was an inspired Labour leader, but over-played his hand and after some preliminary successes his big strike failed. However, during the strike Connolly formed a tiny force of some 200 men, which he called the Irish Citizen Army, to protect the strikers in their clashes with the police. At the end of the strike the little army nearly faded away – but was resuscitated by Sean O'Casey, the playwright, who emerged from the Dublin slums to re-launch the Irish Citizen Army at a meeting in 1914. O'Casey resigned from the Citizen Army shortly afterwards owing to disagreement with Constance Markievicz, née Gore-Booth, of Lissadell, Co. Sligo, who played a dramatic if not very effective part in subsequent events. Larkin's importance in Irish affairs ceased and the direction of the Citizen Army and the Irish trade union movement devolved on Connolly.

But to return to events in Ulster and in Unionist politics. Throughout the latter part of the nineteenth century the Orange Order had been gathering strength as an expression of extreme Protestant and Unionist sentiment. In the election of 1885 Lord Randolph Churchill and Joseph Chamberlain had both sought to mobilize Orange opinion in Ulster against Home

Rule and in favour of the Conservative Party. In the election the Conservatives won 16 seats in Ulster, the Home Rulers 17, and it was this meagre result which led English politicians on the whole to minimize the effectiveness of Unionist determination. The defeat of the bill was marked by serious riots in Belfast. The Protestant shipyard workers attacked the Catholic dockers and 32 people were killed. For twenty years from 1886 little happened in Ulster on the Home Rule front though George Wyndham, the Chief Secretary, was driven from office in 1905 when his Under-Secretary put forward extremely modest proposals for a small degree of self-government for Ireland. But this period marked the rise to prominence of Edward Carson, originally a Dublin lawyer, who had been very useful to A. J. Balfour when Chief Secretary. Carson subsequently moved to the Bar in London, took silk, and became one of the outstanding advocates of his day. But Unionist policy was the 'guiding star of his political life', as he said himself. He was really a southern Unionist but soon saw that the Protestants of Ulster gave him the mass following that was necessary if anything was to be achieved. When the second election of 1910 made it clear that a Home Rule Bill would be introduced, Carson and his ally James Craig, later Lord Craigavon, made it plain that they would resist Home Rule to the extreme limit – and this before any Home Rule Bill had even been drafted. Bonar Law, speaking in Belfast in 1912 to an audience of 100,000 Ulstermen, was hardly less extreme, in spite of the fact that he was leader of one of the two great political parties.

Since 1900 the leader of the Nationalists in Parliament had been John Redmond, a nice man and an excellent speaker. His love of Parliament and its ways was of predominant importance in his outlook. Maintenance of close contact with the political grass roots at home was sacrificed to his enjoyment of the Parliamentary Club. What was remarkable about the Home Rule Bill when published in 1912 and subsequently passed in 1914, was that it was a wishy-washy affair that could hardly be expected to stand the test of time. One could have understood its rejection by Redmond on the ground of its inadequacy, but it is harder to understand its acceptance by Redmond while it was rejected in hysterical terms by the Unionists. Perhaps the Nationalists regarded it as a step in the right direction, albeit an inadequate one, while the Unionists thought any step towards Home Rule was to be resisted to the utmost. That the Conservatives did indeed use the strongest language may be seen from one quotation from Bonar Law in a speech he made at Blenheim Palace in July 1912: 'Even if the Home Rule Bill was carried through the Commons there are things stronger than parliamentary majorities.' He went on to say of the Ulster Protestants: 'If an attempt were made to deprive these men of their birthright – as part of a corrupt parliamentary bargain – they would be justified in resisting such an attempt by all means in their power including force. I can imagine no length of resistance to which Ulster can go in which I should not be prepared to support them.' The 'corrupt parliamentary bargain' was apparently a claim that Home Rule had not been properly presented to the public at the previous election. This was of course preposterous. Home Rule had been official Liberal policy for very many years. It is typical of the sloppy attitude to law and order in this country and in this century that a call to armed rebellion should have been ignored by the authorities.

It is interesting that this first suggestion of the partition of Ulster came from a Liberal M.P., Mr Agar-Robartes, who in June 1912 proposed that the four most Protestant counties should be excluded from Home Rule.

In September 1912 Carson led a huge number of Ulstermen in signing the 'Solemn League and Covenant to use all necessary means to defeat the present conspiracy to set up a Home Rule Parliament in Ireland'. The title of this manifesto was to recall the Scottish League and Covenant of 1638. In Ulster in 1912 Carson claimed to have secured half a million signatures.

In January 1913 was formed the Ulster Volunteer Force, organized and led by an Indian Army general recommended by, of all people, Field-Marshal Lord Roberts. Though the volunteers drilled with dummy rifles, it became known later that year that rifles, machine guns and ammunition for this force were being imported. In November 1913 a corresponding Nationalist army was formed, called the Irish Volunteers. Faced with a deteriorating situation, the government at last took steps to strengthen the naval and military forces in Northern Ireland. This was regarded as a grave step and led in due course in March 1914 to what is known as the Curragh Mutiny. It was not a mutiny, but a group of 58 officers stationed at the Curragh offered their resignations rather than take part in the coercion of Ulster. The whole episode, conducted in a very emotional atmosphere, was very badly handled by the authorities. Sir Henry Wilson and Sir Hubert Gough prevailed on the Secretary of State for War, Sir John Seely, to give a pledge that the army would not be used to crush political opposition to the Home Rule Bill. Asquith subsequently repudiated the pledge and dismissed Sir John Seely but did nothing about the generals mainly concerned.

In April the Ulster Volunteers pulled off a very successful coup, landing large amounts of arms at three northern Irish ports and distributing them all over the Province in twenty-four hours. They had no trouble with the authorities and there were no prosecutions. The natural consequence ensued. The Irish Volunteers sought to equip themselves to be on equal terms with the North.

By June 1914 the situation was deteriorating and it was possible that we were sliding into a civil war which might not be confined to Ireland. The Unionists were determined and armed; King George V was sympathetic to Ulster; Asquith was by then a weak man with a divided Cabinet, and Redmond was a man of peace. The latter two were under great pressure to agree to a compromise and this was what eventually happened – after the outbreak of war with Germany. The Home Rule Bill became law, but with two provisos, first, that it would not come into effect until the end of the war, and second, not until Parliament had been able to consider amending legislation for Ulster.

Asquith was not really interested in Ireland, as his Liberal predecessors, Gladstone and Campbell-Bannerman, had been. No doubt he felt he had got round a difficult corner with some success. The Unionists had in fact won their point. The odd man out was Redmond, who did not seem to have realized that by his weakness he had abandoned the Nationalist cause and left its furtherance to extra-parliamentary forces.

Chapter nine

THE EASTER RISING AND THE TREATY

In the previous few years much had been done to re-suscitate the Irish Republican Brotherhood, which had fallen into elderly and inactive hands. And with this rejuvenation came the recruitment of the Irish Volunteers. The running of guns by the Ulster Volunteers made their rivals in the South feel that they too must be armed, and there ensued one of the more bizarre episodes of recent Irish history. Money was short, but enough was collected by Anglo-Irish sympathizers to buy 1,500 rifles and 45,000 rounds of ammunition in Germany. These were smuggled into Ireland on two private yachts, one piloted by Erskine Childers, the other after two transfers by an eminent Dublin surgeon, Sir Thomas Myles. This operation owed much to Sir Roger Casement, who had been given his K.C.M.G. by the Foreign Office for his work in exposing the exploitation of natives in Peru and the Congo. The operation involved prominent figures: Mrs Stopford Green, daughter of an Archdeacon and widow of the famous historian J. R. Green; Mary Spring Rice, daughter of Lord Monteagle and first cousin of the British Ambassador in Washington; and Erskine Childers, who had fought in the British Army in the Boer War, had been a clerk in the House of Commons and had written the wonderful spy story *The Riddle of the Sands*. One rather gets the impression that these people, with the possible exception of Casement, were no revolutionaries but arranged the whole operation as something of a lark. The arms landed at Howth by Erskine Childers were brought to Dublin by the Irish Volunteers. On the way some of them were intercepted by troops. The troops returning to barracks were baited by a crowd, and there was some shooting, with three killed and a number of wounded. This caused less of an outcry than would otherwise have been the case as it took place at the end of July 1914, a few days before the outbreak of the First War. The gun-running gave a great boost to the recruitment of Volunteers and by September 1914 the force had risen to 180,000.

Redmond had indicated rather vaguely that the Irish Volunteers would be available for the defence of Ireland. However, in this same month of September he unexpectedly delivered a speech in County Wicklow urging the Volunteers to fight in the British Army wherever they were needed. The effect was to split the Volunteers, some nine-tenths following the Redmond line, the remainder coming under the control of the I.R.B. led by Patrick Pearse, Thomas MacDonagh and Joseph Plunkett, all afterwards executed following the Easter Rising of 1916.

Redmond seems to have been under the impression that at the end of the war, which he expected to be brief, the Ulster counties would drop their demand to opt out of Home Rule. This naïve idea was shaken by the composition of the Coalition Government of 1915, which included both Bonar Law and Carson, the protagonists for Ulster. But by then Redmond and his parliamentary party had lost all influence over the course of events.

The leaders of the militant section of the Volunteers were not the political thugs one might have expected. Plunkett was a member of one of the more distinguished Irish families. His father was a Papal Count and director of the National Museum. His health was not good and his main interests had been religious and literary. He was much influenced by the poems of St John of the Cross. MacDonagh was a University lecturer; Pearse's father was an English immigrant. He was himself a barrister. The element these three men had in common, apart from their militant nationalism, was a passionate interest in the Irish language and in Gaelic culture. All three were poets: Pearse ran a school for the teaching of Irish where boys were confronted with a fresco embodying the words of Cuchulain, the legendary hero of Ulster: 'I care not though I were to live but one day and one night, if only my fame and my deeds live after me.' In 1913 he was asked by the I.R.B. to give the memorial Wolfe Tone speech. In it there are two passages worth quoting (from *Ireland Since the Famine*); 'To break the connection with England, the never-failing source of all our political evils, and to assert the independence of my country – these are my objects. To invite the whole people of Ireland to abolish the memory of all past dissensions, and to substitute the common name of Irishman in place of the denominations of Protestant, Catholic and Dissenter.' He moved on to his finishing words: 'Such is the high and sorrowful destiny of the heroes: to turn their backs to the pleasant paths and their faces to the hard paths, to blind their eyes to the fair things of life – and to follow only the far, faint call that leads them into the battle or to the harder death at the foot of a gibbet.'

Between the outbreak of the European War in August 1914 and the Easter Rising in Dublin in 1916 a series of confused and obscure discussions took place Council of the I.R.B. was the most powerful group, but they were so obsessed by the need for security that leading members of the I.R.B. were not allowed to know their plans. Though they were supposed to control the Irish Volunteers, these numbering about 13,000, the commander of the Volunteers was not in their confidence. Meanwhile James Connolly, controlling the 200 members of the Irish Citizen Army, was not a member of the I.R.B. and, unlike the other militants, saw the independence of Ireland only in a Marxist context. In January 1916, however, the situation was changed by the admission of Connolly to the I.R.B. and his agreement to co-operate with the I.R.B. in a rising at Easter. This was not known to Eoin MacNeill, the commander of the Volunteers, whose policy was directly opposed to that of the activists of the I.R.B. MacNeill thought there was no point in a rising unless it had a reasonable chance of success. Pearse and his friends were thinking in terms of propaganda. A rising that led to loss of life would further the cause of Irish Independence regardless of the military success or failure of the venture.

Since 1914 negotiations had taken place with the Germans – partly through Sir Roger Casement, whose intervention was no great help. The Germans were to help with arms and eventually undertook to land arms in Tralee Bay in time for the Easter Rising. This, like almost every part of the organization for that event, was badly bungled and the arms never reached rhe Volunteers. The German ship with the arms indeed reached the Kerry coast from Lübeck, but the boat had no wireless, it was not met by the expected pilot boat nor did it rendezvous with the submarine bringing Casement. It was then intercepted by the Navy and was sunk by the Captain while being escorted into Queenstown.

When this became known in Dublin, MacNeill's reluctance to call out the Volunteers became decisive and he issued orders and published a notice in the *Sunday Independent* that all Volunteer movements were to be abandoned. This meant in practice that the Rising was limited to Dublin and to those units effectively controlled by the Military Council of the I.R.B. From MacNeill's point of view such a puny operation could only lead to the deaths of some brave men without justification. From the I.R.B. leaders' point of view the loss of life would give Irish Nationalism a new impetus, and of course this is what actually happened.

Usually revolutions have as their background an atmosphere of popular discontent. But this was hardly true in the spring of 1916. The country was prosperous – more so than usual. But there was an important fly in the ointment. At the outbreak of war recruitment in Ireland for the British Army had been brisk, but latterly this had fallen away while the casualties in France were appalling. This had led to a degree of conscription in Englnd. Ireland was excluded but conscription there, too, remained in the background as a future possibility.

As Easter 1916 approached it is to be remarked that bungling was not confined to the Irish conspirators. News of the proposed landing of arms in Kerry and of a rising to coincide had reached the Admiralty owing to their success in breaking the German code. But this was not passed on direct to the Irish government, who were mostly concerned. It reached them in a leisurely and roundabout way through the commander of the English Home Forces.

By Easter Day the German arms ship had been sunk, Casement arrested and the Volunteers had been publicly instructed to call off their movements. This seemed to the Viceroy, Lord Wimborne, a good moment to move in and arrest the Nationalist leaders, but Birrell, the Chief Secretary, was in London and after much dithering it was decided to do nothing till Tuesday, by which date events had overtaken them.

The Rising was to start on the morning of Easter Monday. The men involved may have amounted to 1,600 – something over 1,300 Volunteers and rather over 200 Citizen Army. The centre of their operations was to be the General Post Office in O'Connell Street, where the formation of the 'Provisional Government of the Irish Republic' was proclaimed. The proclamation was signed by seven men, Thomas Clarke, Sean Mac-Dermott, Patrick Pearse, James Connolly, Thomas MacDonagh, Edmund Kent and Joseph Plunkett. The G.P.O. was the centre of operations, but large buildings were siezed in other parts of the city. A group under Eamonn de Valera, until recently President of the Irish Republic, occupied Bolands Bakery. Most of the casualties were caused at the Mount Street Bridge, where a small group of Volunteers inflicted severe casualties on the Sherwood Foresters. The Rising lasted five days, and was ended by shellfire from the gunboat *Helga* and by spreading fire. Much damage was done and the total casualties were officially put at 1,350 killed and severely wounded, a figure that was

to include both civilian and military losses. On the sur-
render of Pearse and the insurgents a number of them
were tried and sentenced to death or to long terms of
imprisonment. Fifteen were actually shot, Casement
was hanged; the other prisoners were released after
serving only a few months. The outcry in Ireland and
elsewhere then and since about the brutality of the
sentences has been greatly overdone. While sympathiz-
ing with men who gave their lives in a cause in which
they passionately believed, I see no sense in glossing over
the fact that from the British point of view this was
armed rebellion in time of war. For such an enterprise
to end in fifteen executions is extremely lenient by the
standards set elsewhere. Casement had been landed by
submarine, his conduct throughout the war was treason-
able and I cannot really see that his admirers can
reasonably feel he was unjustly treated.

The reaction to the Rising was at first hostile, not
only of course in England, but in Ireland, too. But it
soon became apparent that the effect of the Rising was
to cut away the ground under the feet of Redmond
and the Home Rule Party in the House of Commons.
The future of Irish politics lay outside the parliamentary sphere.

However, one last effort was made by Lloyd George
in 1916 to arrive at an immediate and agreed solution
to the Home Rule problem. Separate negotiations were
carried out with Redmond and his Home Rulers on
the one hand and with Carson and his Unionists on
the other. Home Rule was to be granted as soon as
possible for the 26 southern counties; Redmond was
given to understand that the exclusion of the 6 Ulster
counties would be temporary; Carson was assured the

exclusion would be permanent. Even this deal was repudiated by Lord Lansdowne, a leader of the traditional Protestant Ascendancy in Ireland. The negotiations came to nothing, but Redmond's authority in Ireland was fatally compromised. His brother was killed in action in France, where his son, too, was fighting. He died in 1918 of what may have amounted to a broken heart.

To emphasize the point that nationalism had deserted the parliamentary path for more violent courses, came the result of a by-election in January 1917. Count Plunkett, the father of Joseph Plunkett, executed a few months earlier, stood in North Roscommon against the official Home Rule candidate and won easily. Later in the year three more by-elections were won by Sinn Fein candidates, one of them de Valera, who stood for East Clare immediately on his release from prison.

The government in these months was pursuing a policy of half-hearted coercion. In the course of a hunger strike, one hunger-striker, Thomas Ashe, was forcibly fed and subsequently died. His funeral was a big propaganda occasion attended by a huge crowd and an escort of armed volunteers, who fired a volley over the grave. The only speaker was Michael Collins, who made a public appearance for the first time. He was a member of the I.R.B. and had these words to say – referring to the volley of rifle fire – 'Nothing additional remains to be said. The volley which we have just heard is the only speech which it is proper to make above the grave of a dead Fenian.'

Michael Collins was then twenty-seven and had been a member of the I.R.B. for eight years. He had been in the fighting at the G.P.O. He was efficient, ruthless and a first-class fighting man.

It was at this time that the division between the I.R.B. and other militant groups began – a division which was to bedevil nationalist politics for a long time to come. While three of the top men in the Volunteers were I.R.B., the Chief of Staff, Cathal Brugha, was anti-I.R.B. Brugha thought that the Easter Rising had been botched because of secret moves by the I.R.B. conflicting with orders given by others. Surely there should only be one nationalist movement without a secret power centre. De Valera was President of Sinn Fein and of the Volunteers but had only briefly been a member of the I.R.B. and was so no longer. De Valera's reason was that all secret societies were condemned by the Catholic Church and so he had not rejoined the Brotherhood after his release from prison.

After the by-elections the next big event in the Nationalist Campaign was in the spring of 1918 when a Conscription Bill was brought in which could be applied to Ireland by Order in Council. This united all Irish political groups from Cardinal Logue to de Valera. The political emotion was still further enhanced by the replacement of Lord Wimborne as Viceroy by Sir John French, later Lord Ypres. As a general he was sent to pursue a tougher policy. The tougher policy was limited to imprisoning known Sinn Fein leaders, which the Sinn Feiners themselves seemed to welcome as good propaganda for their cause. Nevertheless it would have been unwise to let all the leaders be caught. Collins and Brugha were not found by the police and remained outside to organize resistance – and above all an intelligence service which was to prove so valuable to Collins in the years ahead.

The obliteration of the old Irish party came in November 1918. Prior to the General Election in that month Redmond's old party had 68 seats, sundry independents 10, Unionists 18 and Sinn Fein 7. The result of the election was: Sinn Fein 73, Unionists 25, the old Irish party 6. The Sinn Fein members refused to take their seats at Westminster but regarded themselves as members of the parliament of an independent Ireland and as such, those who were available to do so, formed the first Dail in Dublin in January 1919.

It was about the same time that the first shots were fired in what became an Anglo-Irish war. Two policemen were escorting a supply of explosives to a quarry in Tipperary. They were ambushed and killed. The killing was not part of the intention, but was followed in later months by other similar incidents in which policemen and a magistrate were murdered. It should be mentioned that the Royal Irish Constabulary, the Irish police, were, and had for long been, an armed force. Throughout 1919 the attacks on the police continued and in the last eight months of the year eighteen policemen were killed. Towards the end of the year a number of successful attacks were made on detectives who had shown too great a knowledge of the I.R.A. and its affairs. This was extended in 1920 to the murder of an elderly magistrate in Dublin who had been too successful in tracking down I.R.A. funds under different names lodged in the banks. What may have been the first reprisal took place in March 1920 when the Mayor of Cork was murdered by masked gunmen. The I.R.A. believed this to be the work of the police and in due course shot down the police inspector believed to be responsible.

While events in Ireland were proceeding on a course of escalating violence the British Government brought in the Government of Ireland Bill. This was the Act that created Stormont. It was to have been matched by a similar parliament in Dublin bridged by a Council of Ireland. The whole concept was completely divorced from reality and as far as the 26 counties were concerned was merely ignored.

There were ugly riots in the North, mainly in Londonderry and Belfast, in which Catholic families were attacked by Protestant mobs. The attacks were not unprovoked but led to 62 deaths. Meanwhile in the South the police were reinforced by the Black and Tans. They were called after a well-known hunt in the south of Ireland and so named as there was inadequate police equipment and they wore khaki uniforms with police caps and belts. They were joined by a new body called the Auxiliary Division of the Royal Irish Constabulary. These new forces were recruited from men who had fought in the trenches and to whom life and property were of small account. They came to behave as if every man's hand in Ireland was raised against them, and they were not far wrong. In the period 1920–21 there seem to have been about 14,000 police in Ireland and some 26,000 troops. The total force of the I.R.A. was said to be about 15,000, but Michael Collins, their Commander, who should have known, put the active element as low as 3,000. In 1920 the casualties among the police were 176 killed and of soldiers 54. It was thought about 43 I.R.A. men were killed in the same period.

As 1920 drew to a close the war took the form of assassination followed by reprisals, mostly by the Black and Tans. This period of terror and counter-terror led to a culmination in County Cork in December 1920. Two ambushes of police had caused many deaths. A few days later Auxiliaries and Black and Tans poured into the City of Cork and burnt down the centre of the town. This reprisal was of course unauthorized and the men mostly drunk.

It is a curious aspect of the politics of that time that while events were pursuing their violent course in Ireland, de Valera spent eighteen months in the United States drumming up support for the Nationalist cause. In his absence the Presidency was held first by Griffith and subsequently by Michael Collins. De Valera did indeed elicit much sympathy from his Irish-American audiences and also collected substantial sums of money. His attempts to secure political support were not successful but the 4 million dollars despatched to Ireland did much to keep the I.R.A. in the field.

In November 1920 Griffith was arrested and this seems to have decided de Valera to return to Ireland, which he did at the end of December. Though the guerrilla warfare continued unabated, it was growing apparent that English public opinion was becoming increasingly unhappy over the excesses committed in their name. De Valera's return to Ireland seemed to provide an opportunity for a fresh start. However, when de Valera met Lord Derby and later Sir James Craig in May 1921, the result was entirely negative. In the elections that took place under the new Government of Ireland Act, Craig and his Unionists secured 40 out of 52 seats in the Six Counties, while in the South republican candidates won every seat unopposed except for the four seats representing Trinity College, Dublin, which went to Independents. In the South the new members had no intention of implementing the Act, but the election was regarded as selecting members for the second Dail.

Under the terms of the relevant act, if less than half the members showed up on the appointed day, the act would lapse and the 26 counties would be governed as a Crown Colony. The military estimates were that under these circumstances the troops necessary to maintain law and order would number at least 80,000 and probably more.

At this point a number of different factors converged to bring about a new situation. Lloyd George had been pondering a settlement on the lines of giving the 26 counties Dominion status, George V made a speech in Belfast, partly drafted by Smuts, urging conciliation – and perhaps most important of all, the I.R.A. was running out of arms. Michael Collins afterwards declared that he could not have kept going for more than another three weeks. Anyway the result was a truce from July 11th, 1921. De Valera insisted on meeting Lloyd George alone in spite of advice he had from Sir James Craig, who warned him: 'You must be mad. Take a witness, Lloyd George will give any account of the interview that comes into his mind or that suits him.' The warning was not heeded, though with advantage it might have been.

As a result of the negotiations Southern Ireland was offered Dominion status while claiming complete independence. Individual points that were difficult for Nationalists to swallow were a recognition of the powers and privileges of the government in Stormont, a limitation on the Irish Army and the grant of naval and air bases for British forces. However, after discussion in Dublin it was agreed to send delegates to London 'to ascertain how the association of Ireland with the community of nations known as the British empire may best be reconciled with Irish national aspirations'. For reasons that do not appear, de Valera was not one of the delegates. In fact the delegation under-represented the extreme Republican faction and was given terms of reference that were contradictory and which were to lead to much trouble later. The two chief Irish negotiators were Arthur Griffith and Michael Collins, while on the other side were all the British big guns from Lloyd George to Birkenhead and Churchill.

As the negotiations progressed the two sticking points were Ulster and the exact status of the King. Both sides seem to have attached a large – and irrational – importance to this latter constitutional point, which in the eventual outcome can be seen to be secondary while the position of Ulster was in fact central. The Irish delegates seem to have thought that Ulster could be coerced into joining an independent Ireland. This had not been politically possible in 1914, why should it have been possible in 1921? However, Lloyd George suggested a Boundary Commission. The implication was that Catholic areas would be detached from the Six Counties and made over to the Dublin Administration. The Irish negotiators assumed that such a Commission would reduce the Six Counties to four or less, which would not then constitute a viable entity. Eventually on December 6th, 1921, the Treaty was signed under which Southern Ireland assumed Dominion status and shared common citizenship with the United Kingdom. The delegates signed without reference back to Dublin and did not even communicate with their colleagues by telephone. Though they had been given plenipotentiary powers, they were also expected to check with Dublin before signing the Treaty. The fact that the instructions were contradictory and that de Valera was in Dublin, not London, led to tragic consequences in Ireland which have not yet been entirely dissipated.

When the delegates returned to Dublin their signature of the Treaty was confirmed in the Irish Cabinet by a majority of one – with de Valera in the minority. He immediately issued a statement that the Treaty was not acceptable. After a long debate in the Dail extended over many days the Treaty was approved by 64 votes to 57. Nearly the whole of the discussion was about the exact status of independent Ireland. Partition played a very small part in the debate. The reason seems to have been that Collins was convinced after discussions in London with Churchill and Birkenhead that the Six Counties would certainly be reduced to Four and that such a small enclave would not be viable.

Following on the debate, de Valera and his followers withdrew from the Dail and Griffith was elected President in his place.

Unfortunately the division in the ranks of the politicians was paralleled by divisions in the ranks of the I.R.A. While Collins and the I.R.B. were on the side of the Treaty, de Valera, Cathal Brugha and many of the top army commanders were against. The anti-Treaty elements in the country were encouraged by de Valera to take up arms and the anti-Treaty officers held a convention at which leaders of the Irregulars were chosen. This was followed shortly afterwards by the occupation of the Four Courts and other Dublin buildings, and by similar action throughout the country. Collins was in a desperately tight corner, negotiating with de Valera on the one hand and a very sceptical British Government on the other, while the Irregulars were fortifying strongpoints in Dublin and replenishing their funds by robbing banks.

While the issue of civil war was still in the balance, elections to the parliament of self-governing Ireland were held. The result was 58 seats out of 128 went to pro-Treaty men, 35 to anti-Treaty candidates, the remainder being various splinter groups of which Labour and Farmers were the most important. Simultaneously Field-Marshal Sir Henry Wilson, who had just been appointed military adviser to Craig, was assassinated in London. It is not clear who ordered the assassination, but it was most probably Michael Collins, angered by the anti-Catholic riots in the North. These had caused the deaths of 544 people in the years 1920–22 and led to some thousands fleeing south. The Protestant rioters were not without some provocation, but the deaths and damage to property were overwhelmingly the result of attacks by Protestant mobs on Catholics.

At this the British Government's patience ran out and Collins was warned that his Government could not be taken seriously unless it cleared up the pockets of resistance in Dublin and elsewhere. In particular, the occupation of the Four Courts must be brought to an end – as it was, with the aid of artillery lent by the British Army. Brugha, de Valera and Countess Markievicz (the two latter had been condemned to death after the Easter Rising) joined the Irregulars. At first they occupied fixed points in Dublin and Cork but when they were shelled out of these they moved on to guerrilla warfare in the country. Collins was the better general and though he was killed in the fighting it was his leadership and his control of the I.R.B. that led to victory for the pro-Treaty forces.

Irish politics are not always easy to understand and this must have been one of the most incomprehensible episodes in Irish history. The Irish negotiators had in fact got all the essentials of independence and the only fly in the ointment was the Government in the North-East. But the civil war which raged in Ireland from the summer of 1922 to the summer of 1923 was not over the partition of Ireland, but over whether the Nationalists should have accepted anything short of a Republic. The war was a bloody affair which left its mark down to the present day. The Fianna Fail Party of Mr Lynch is descended from the anti-Treaty party while Fine Gael is the offspring of the pro-Treaty party. It is a valid criticism of Dublin politics that they have not yet entirely escaped from the stale politics and misconceived issues of fifty years ago.

Chapter ten

IRELAND AFTER THE TREATY

The South

Though the war ended in May 1923, this was by no means the end of conflict and bitterness. De Valera set up a rival government, while the legal government was weakened by the death of Griffith at the early age of fifty and Collins's death in action. Erskine Childers was tried and shot and when a pro-Treaty deputy was assassinated four Republicans were shot in reprisal. This policy of reprisal was continued and the total so killed eventually amounted to 77.

De Valera and his followers refused to take their seats in the Dail, which elected W. T. Cosgrave as Prime Minister in the place of Arthur Griffith. Cosgrave was the father of the present Prime Minister. His Minister of Home Affairs was Kevin O'Higgins, one of the more remarkable figures in the Irish politics of those days. He was only thirty-one and seems to have been a strange mixture of gaiety and ruthlessness. One of the reprisal killings on his orders was that of Rory O'Connor, who a few weeks earlier had been best man at O'Higgins's own wedding. O'Higgins was himself assassinated in 1927. It was some two or three years after the end of the civil war before the country got back to normal and it was not until 1927 that de Valera and his followers, now under the banner of Fianna Fail, took part in the normal political activities of the country.

It may be recalled that the Treaty provided that if the Six Counties opted out of a United Ireland, a Boundary Commission would be set up to 'determine, in accordance with the wishes of the inhabitants, so far as may be compatible with economic and geographic conditions, the boundaries between Northern Ireland and the rest of Ireland.' In 1924 the Commission was set up, consisting of a South African judge as independent Chairman, an Ulsterman appointed by the British government when Craig refused to make a nomination, and another Ulsterman, a Catholic, nominated by the Dublin government. When the Treaty was signed Lloyd George gave Collins and his fellow negotiators to understand that the Boundary Commission would allocate large areas at least of Fermanagh and Tyrone to the South. In the outcome, the Commission seems to have been on the point of recommending the transfer of a chunk of Donegal to the North. The whole episode reads as if Eoin Mac-Neill, the southern Irish representative, had been taken for a ride. Perhaps he assumed from the start that the outcome would be favourable to his government and did not keep in touch with the thinking of his two fellow-Commissioners. In the end the Commission never published its report, the boundary was left as it was and the Irish Free State was relieved of its financial liabilities under the Treaty. No doubt the financial settlement softened the disappointment, but on this occasion, as before, the Irish were bound to feel that they had been tricked.

In June 1927 elections were held in which de Valera's new party, Fianna Fail, won 44 seats against Cosgrave's party's 47. As de Valera and nearly all his followers refused to take the oath, Cosgrave continued in office and introduced a bill to make every candidate swear to take the oath and his seat if elected. If he did not do so his seat was to be declared vacant and he himself was to be disqualified. This became law and caused de Valera to perform one of his more spectacular feats of casuistry. It is not for nothing he has been called the constitutional Houdini of his generation. He found that after all he could sign the oath which was now an empty political formula. The result of the Fianna Fail members taking their seats was that with their allies they had the same number of votes as the Government Coalition. This necessitated a second General Election three months after the last, in which the two main parties gained seats while the smaller parties all lost. Mr Cosgrave, the Farmers and some independents formed the government which remained in office until 1932.

Though de Valera and his Fianna Fail had become constitutionalists, this did not mean that all the old militants had beaten their rifles into ploughshares. Lemass, afterwards Prime Minister, described Fianna Fail as 'a slightly constitutional party', and at times it appeared in public with members of one or other of the illegal military organizations. After 1928, when the Public Safety Act of 1927 was repealed, crimes of violence began to increase, with much intimidation of juries, and this reached a dangerous level in 1931. Hitherto the military organizations had been mainly nationalist, but with the onset of the Depression from 1929 they tended to acquire a tinge of Marxism, and it is this distinction that accounts for the difference between the Official I.R.A. in 1973, which is more or less Marxist, and the Provisional I.R.A., which is not.

The Officials' policy goes back to 1929, while the policy of the Provisionals is a reversion to a still earlier purpose.

When the General Election came in 1932, Cosgrave and his party had been in office for ten years, they had just passed a ferocious Public Safety Act, which was violently unpopular in Republican circles, and they were involved in all the economic troubles of the Great Depression. It was not surprising that they lost the election to de Valera and his coalition with the Labour Party. What was surprising was that de Valera was to remain in office for the next sixteen years.

Fortified by another General Election a few months later, de Valera set about dismantling the Treaty – at any rate in its more legalistic aspects. The Oath was done away with; a new Governor-General without powers, a Mr Buckley, was installed in a suburban villa; payment on Land Annuities to the British Government was stopped, the right of appeal to the Judicial Committee of the Privy Council was abolished. These moves had become legally possible owing to the passing of the Statute of Westminster in 1931, which of course was meant to clarify the relations between the United Kingdom and all the Dominions and had no special reference to Ireland.

The Abdication at the end of 1936 gave Mr de Valera a further opportunity of emphasizing the independence of Ireland. In the new constitution of 1937 Ireland became a Republic in fact though not in name. The fact that Ireland was not called a Republic seems to have been due to two considerations. The first was that the name of Republic could only properly be applied to all 32 counties and the second was that any such declaration at that time would have hardened the attitude of the Unionists.

These various legal changes were taken pretty calmly by the British government, but the refusal to pay the Land Annuities led to an economic war which lasted altogether about six years. On the whole trans-action Ireland was financially the loser. However, in 1938 the economic war was brought to an end and for no apparent reason Chamberlain threw into the agreement the naval bases in Southern Ireland held by British forces under the Treaty. That Chamber-lain should have done this when a European War was clearly becoming a dangerous probability is one of the more irresponsible actions of that lamentable man. When the war did break out, the neutrality of Southern Ireland and unavailability of the bases created fresh bitterness between Northern and Southern Ireland but gave the more nationalistic Irish the feeling that now they were really independent. They presumably did not look to the possibility of a British defeat and the subsequent rule of a Gauleiter in Dublin.

One would have thought that with the coming to office and to power of de Valera the old antagonisms would die down, if not out. But Irish politics are not as simple as that and memories are long. When de Valera took office all I.R.A. detainees were released. They were, after all, de Valera's political allies. But instead of going home and going about their normal business they started recruiting new members and drilling them. This naturally led to equivalent action by the Cosgrave forces, culminating in a semi-Fascist force of Blue Shirts. The latter were more easily identified and were proscribed. The I.R.A. pursued a policy of increasing violence until in 1936 they too were proscribed. Some steam was let off by both sides when they departed to the Spanish Civil War. It is said that some 300 supported the Republicans while 700 Blue Shirts supported Franco.

In 1938 Sean Russell, Chief of Staff of the I.R.A., despatched an Ultimatum to the British Government demanding withdrawal from the Six Counties. This message was, of course, ignored and was followed by explosions over a wide area of England. These were mostly in letter-boxes and public lavatories, but one went off in a crowded street in Coventry and killed five people. The idea of the campaign was apparently to advertise the existence of the I.R.A. and to bring home to British opinion the resentment felt in Ireland over partition. Any effect of the campaign could only have been counter-productive. It carried on in a spasmodic fashion until the summer of 1939.

When war broke out de Valera's government was deeply committed to neutrality. There was much discussion in the British Cabinet whether or not to take important naval bases by force. In the end bases in Northern Ireland were found to be sufficient. In 1944 the American government favoured similar action, but in the end it was thought wiser to let things be. Though southern Ireland was neutral 50,000 persons volunteered to serve in the British forces.

The I.R.A. was not quite inactive and a German named Goertz was parachuted into Ireland in 1940 to organize their activities. He was appalled by the disarray in which he found the rebel forces and told them: 'You know how to die for Ireland, but how to fight for it you have no idea.' Goertz was arrested a few months later and committed suicide in 1947 when about to be deported to Germany. Raids were made on Northern Ireland to no significant effect and during the whole war period twenty-six I.R.A. men lost their lives in one way or another.

Mr de Valera continued in office until the General Election of 1948. His party was still the largest but he was defeated by an improbable coalition of all the minority parties under the Premiership of Mr John Costello, leader of the Fine Gael, the major party governing the Irish Republic at the present time. Mr Costello's coalition included ten deputies under the leadership of Sean McBride (son of W. B. Yeats's love, Maud Gonne) who were more republican even than Mr de Valera. It was to keep these men in line that Mr Costello decided to do away with the External Relations Act and establish the Republic. This, of course, made no real difference to the status of the Irish government, but the consequent act at Westminster included a proviso that Northern Ireland could never be detached from the United Kingdom without the consent of the Northern Irish legislature. Not being a Dublin politician, it is difficult for me to understand this insistence on words, status and legalisms while allowing the real issue, the re-unification of Ireland – or at any rate insistence on the treatment of Northern Catholics as full citizens of their Province – to go by default.

The next episode in Irish political history that has a bearing on Anglo-Irish affairs was in 1951. Dr Browne, the Minister of Health, brought in what has been called the 'mother and child scheme' to benefit without means test mothers and their children up to the age of sixteen. Though Dr Browne was a doctor, his fellow physicians viewed the scheme as an approach to socialized medicine. This difficulty could have been overcome, but the Catholic bishops saw in the scheme an invasion by the State into the intimacies of family life. Dr Browne thought he had overcome the religious objections but there was a succession of misunderstandings. In the outcome the Hierarchy condemned the scheme, Dr Browne had to resign and in the subsequent election the all-party coalition lost its majority and de Valera once more took office. The importance of this episode was that, by the contemporary standards in other countries, Dr Browne's scheme was a reasonable one. But it conflicted with the ideas at that time of the Catholic bishops and so was rejected. In a conflict between Church and State it was made all too clear which side would win in Dublin. If the Unionists in Ulster wanted confirmation of their belief that Home Rule means Rome Rule they had in this controversy the perfect illustration for their purpose. When I mentioned this event to Dr Ryan, the very enlightened Archbishop of Dublin, he said that even the Hierarchy learns from its mistakes. So I think in any similar situation in the future the bishops would tread much more warily.

Mr de Valera's government was a minority one and pursued an undistinguished course for three years until the General Election of 1954, which led to another coalition government under Mr Costello. This had less glamour than its predecessor, as Dr Browne was obviously not now available and Sean McBride refused to serve. Both this government and its predecessor had had difficult economic conditions to contend with and

Mr McBride's position on the sidelines was no help. The result was a revival of the I.R.A., with raids on barracks in Northern Ireland and also in England. Money began to come in from sources in America as well as in Ireland. Mr Costello's attempts to cope with the situation were unsuccessful and in 1957 there was another election, won decisively by Mr de Valera, though it was significant that four constituencies were won by the I.R.A. However, these members refused to take their seats.

Mr de Valera on taking office once more showed a very firm hand in dealing with the I.R.A. This and a rising tide of prosperity brought an end to the I.R.A. campaign which was finally called off in 1962. Mr de Valera retired to the Presidency in 1959 and was replaced as Prime Minister by Mr Lemass, who had been one of the rebels in the General Post Office in 1916, and had fought in the Civil War on the anti-Treaty side. In due course he was succeeded in office by Mr Jack Lynch until he was defeated in the General Election of 1973, by which time Fianna Fail had been in power for thirteen consecutive years.

The Six Counties

While the history of the south of Ireland from 1922 to 1968 had proceeded along a course of growing independence, in Northern Ireland the tendency had been in the opposite direction. The financial arrangements between Stormont and Westminster were frequently modified and each time to the great advantage of the Ulstermen. At first it had been assumed there would be a contribution by the Six Counties to the Imperial

Exchequer but over the years and particularly after the War the contribution was large and in the opposite direction. The idea was that welfare payments in Northern Ireland should be the same as those in England and any deficit was met from London. This of course has had a considerable political effect as the welfare payments in Northern Ireland are much more generous than those in the South. This is of particular benefit to Catholics, who tend to be poorer than the Protestant majority. To agitate for a united Ireland is all very well but if it were achieved on the present basis it would mean a severe loss of income to large numbers of Nationalists in the North. Because of the large and growing contribution to the Province the Stormont government had to agree to a large measure of financial supervision from Whitehall. In spite of this fact, and in spite of the fact that the final authority for the government of Northern Ireland rested with the House of Commons, almost no interest was displayed in Irish affairs for years on end. In one period of just over a year from 1934 to 1935 the House of Commons devoted one hour and fifty minutes to the affairs of Northern Ireland and this figure was by no means abnormal. Furthermore governments in London of the various complexions that ruled from 1922 to 1968 did nothing at all to check the gerrymandering in local authority elections and the gross discrimination in government employment against Catholics. As an instance of the former one can cite the case of the Londonderry City Council. The population included a substantial Catholic majority but the ward boundaries were so drawn as to produce a safe Protestant majority on the Council. In County Fermanagh there are equal numbers of Catholics and Protestants, yet in recent years there have been 35 Unionist councillors to 17 non-Unionist ones. In the matter of jobs one cannot do better than quote Mr John Andrews in 1933 – then Home Minister, and afterwards Prime Minister: 'Another allegation which is made against the Government which is untrue is that of the 31 porters at Stormont 28 are Roman Catholic. I have investigated the matter and I have found that there are 30 Protestants and only one Roman Catholic – there only temporarily.'

An additional move to strengthen the hold of the Unionists on the government at all levels was the abolition of proportional representation in local government in 1922 and in provincial elections in 1929. The purpose of all the discrimination against the Catholics was to ensure a measure of emigration that would leave the Protestant majority at its previous level – and in this way Unionist policy was successful in defeating the higher differential fertility of the Catholics.

When reading about Northern Ireland one cannot help being struck by the *immobilisme* of their affairs. Craig, by then Lord Craigavon, died in office in 1940. Two of his Cabinet Ministers had been in office with him since 1922. Craig's successor Sir Basil Brooke, afterwards Lord Brookeborough, was Prime Minister for twenty years. These men seemed to have learnt nothing, though they may have forgotten the belief in 1922 that the Irish settlement was a temporary affair – the best that could be thought up to end the killing. No one at that time thought it would last fifty years.

Chapter eleven

IRELAND TODAY

The end of the halcyon days of Ulster Unionism and the first beginning of the current era of violence can safely be dated to 1963, the year Terence O'Neill, now Lord O'Neill of the Maine, became Prime Minister in succession to Lord Brookeborough. He has been accused of regarding rank and file members of his party as mere serfs, and he is indeed a member of the landed aristocracy with a long and honourable pedigree. This is no great help in this day and age. He realized that a continuance of the old policy of repression could not be maintained any longer and began a more moderate approach to the problems of his Province, but he mightily offended members of his party by meeting Mr Lemass, at that time Prime Minister of the Republic. Lord O'Neill's policy was undoubtedly right but he should have made sure of adequate support in his party for the moves he was contemplating. This he did not do and after a frustrating period in office he was succeeded by Mr Chichester-Clark, now Lord Moyola, by which time the situation was getting out of control of ministers in Stormont and was being dumped in the lap of the government in London.

To revert to the year 1963. It was in that year that Mrs McCluskey, Catholic wife of a doctor in Dungannon, succeeded by a peaceful demonstration in securing for badly housed Catholics in the town accommodation in some empty houses. The McCluskeys went on to found the Campaign for Social Justice.

In 1966 Protestant gunmen, looking for a well-known member of the I.R.A. and failing to find him, shot and killed a young Catholic barman. Though the three men responsible were convicted of murder and sentenced to life imprisonment, they were held in honour by their Orange Lodge, though not by the Unionist Prime Minister.

In 1967 the Northern Ireland Civil Rights Association was founded and in the following year made an issue of the award of a council house to a young unmarried Protestant girl, secretary of a Unionist politician. The house was in the village of Caledon in the district of Dungannon, and Catholic squatters were evicted from the house to make room for Miss Beattie. A protest march was organized and unexpectedly attracted a crowd of 4,000 people. The Civil Rights Association may have had only limited objectives, or they may have realized that it would be much easier to arouse interest in England over housing allocations than over more specifically nationalist objectives. Members of the I.R.A. were included among the founders of the Association but do not seem to have dominated it, although leading Unionists, led by William Craig, then Minister of Home Affairs, denounced the Association as a front for the I.R.A. The demands made by the Association were six: 1, one man one vote in local elections; 2, the removal of gerrymandered boundaries; 3, laws against discrimination by local government; 4, allocation of public housing on a points system; 5, repeal of the Special Powers Act;

6, disbanding of the part-time 'B' Specials. Lord Cameron in his report on the disturbances commented that 'these reforms were not such as in any sense to endanger the stability of the constitution'.

Following on the successful Dungannon march, one was planned for Londonderry – a much more emotive site for such a demonstration. This was banned by the authorities but took place none the less, until broken up by police baton charges in which Gerry Fitt, a Westminster M.P., was injured. Further demonstrations were held by students and others. The situation was clearly warming up. O'Neill, with a disunited Cabinet, was hoping to head off trouble by suitable concessions to the Catholics; Craig was all for opposing any demands from any Catholics; the C.R.A. with I.R.A. backing felt they were making headway and Brian Faulkner, an old political enemy of O'Neill's, was looking for an opportunity to forward his political career.

In November 1968 there was a big Catholic and Civil Rights procession in Londonderry which led to a serious degree of rioting shown on television screens throughout the United Kingdom. After this it was no longer possible to regard the affairs of Northern Ireland as the private preserve of the Stormont government. By agreement with Mr Wilson and James Callaghan, the Home Secretary, O'Neill announced various reforms of which the principal were the allocation of housing on a points system, the replacement of the gerrymandered borough council of Londonderry and a promise to reform local government and the franchise. This did more to alert the Unionists than to satisfy the Catholics and a proposed Civil Rights march in Armagh was frustrated by large numbers of Protestants led by Dr Paisley.

In January 1969 left-wing elements calling themselves People's Democracy decided to stage a 75-mile march from Belfast to Londonderry. The marchers reached the village of Claudy, about eight miles from Londonderry, and rested there for the night. The I.R.A. set up road-blocks round the village as they had heard reports of impending violence, but these armed men dispersed in the early morning. Meanwhile Protestant groups were assembling, piles of stones were collected, white armbands distributed. When morning came the marchers were attacked at the Burntollet Bridge by a hail of stones and bottles. Many of the assailants were 'B' Specials, evidently on the friendliest terms with the police, who did little to protect the 500 marchers, some of whom were beaten senseless and one girl very nearly killed. This riot was followed by the invasion of the Bogside, a Catholic area of Londonderry, by the police, who roamed through the area causing much damage and inflicting injuries on 163 people who had to be treated in hospital. The effect of these two episodes which, in accordance with Unionist practice, were related, was to convince the Catholic population that the police were their enemies. Mr Faulkner's resignation from Mr O'Neill's cabinet at this point was timed to cause the Prime Minister the maximum of embarrassment. The grounds offered for the resignation were dismissed with contempt by Mr O'Neill.

O'Neill had one last shot in his locker. He called a General Election to re-establish his authority. However, the election did not go well for him, and when he subsequently resigned he was replaced in 1969 by Mr Chichester-Clark, who beat Mr Faulkner for the Premiership by one vote. In the ensuing period of mounting tension the British government seem to have taken a fairly complacent attitude and the new Ulster Prime Minister saw no objection to the traditional Orange Order marches taking place as usual. These led to intensive rioting particularly in the small town of Dungiven. The rioting was more than the Royal Ulster Constabulary could cope with and recourse was had to the 'B' Specials. This was a body of armed Protestant militia. They were given some drill and some weapon training and any volunteers for the force were accepted as long as they were Protestants without a criminal record. They were given no instruction in police work nor had they any legal training of any kind.

Mr Wilson's administration came into office in 1964 but in the first five years only one minister, Sir Frank Soskice, visited Northern Ireland and that for only an afternoon. Mr O'Neill came to London from time to time and had four discussions with Wilson and three with the Home Secretary. The policy pursued while O'Neill was in office was to keep Ulster at arm's length while pressing O'Neill for reform. This policy continued even though from 1966 onwards the possible need for British troops for the maintenance of law and order had been under discussion between Stormont and London. Nevertheless until 1968 the Home Office had no official concerned whole time with the affairs of Northern Ireland. These formed part of the General Department of the Home Office, which is concerned with London taxis, among other things.

It was in August 1969 that the balloon really went up when the Catholic areas of Londonderry came under siege. The Catholics were not blameless in the disorder but the real villains of the piece were the R.U.C. Large-scale riots over several days in Londonderry were followed by an ugly episode in Armagh. These disorders were compounded by savage rioting in Belfast. In the past Belfast had often remained fairly quiet in times of political tension as the Catholics were outnumbered and isolated in ghettos. At any rate for this reason any provocation was likely to be by the Protestants. This time it would be difficult to say who provoked what, but the R.U.C. called out their armoured cars fitted with machine guns. Much of the damage and many of the casualties were caused by misunderstanding and confusion. But in the outcome there were ten killed, and one Catholic street was burned to the ground as well as other Catholic premises. It was in this riot that British troops were called in for the first time. There were too few and they were called in too late. The lack of foresight and preparation by the British authorities was due to an extreme reluctance to be involved in Irish affairs although it was the British government and not the Cabinet in Stormont who were the final authority responsible for maintaining law and order in the Six Counties.

The reaction of the British government was to act in ways that would produce immediate results and leave more far-reaching changes for later. The reform that struck them as most immediate was the disbanding of the 'B' Specials and placing the police under the command of the army. Discrimination in housing, gerrymandering and proportional representation were lower priorities. Mr Callaghan, the Home Secretary and so the Minister for Northern Ireland, paid a visit to Belfast and made a favourable impression as a professional politician, unlike his Stormont counterparts. Mr Callaghan has the advantage of an Irish Catholic name, though he was born in Portsmouth and sits for a Welsh constituency. He has a statesmanlike appearance, which was a help to him on his Irish visits. One gets the impression that none of the Labour ministers concerned knew Ireland or had read any Irish history. If they had, surely they would have been far more alarmed than they were over the outbreak of serious violence. It would have been plain to them that this was not trouble over housing allocation but a re-opening of the political and sectarian warfare that had marred Irish history for centuries. 'Choosing the least disturbing option', which was said to be Mr Wilson's policy at the time, was no way to settle political strife that in one form or another had been in progress for eight hundred years. To call for Lord Hunt to report on the police and Lord Cameron on one set of riots and Mr Justice Scarman on another and later series was no solution to anything. These inquiries are usually instituted to gain time, but already there was no time to lose. And both ministers and civil servants thought in terms of administrative reforms, while the problems were deep-seated political ones. In any case in a situation where grievances had been allowed to fester too long, Catholics were likely to expect results to be far sooner in evidence than was politically or constitutionally possible.

Meanwhile the army, originally numbering 2,500, had been stepped up to 6,000. Its use for police work was risky. The troops had neither been recruited nor trained for this work. They were originally called in mainly to protect the Catholics, but in the normal course of maintaining law and order they seemed to be supporting the status quo – the Orange status quo. Even the legal right to intervene was in some doubt. Unless the correct procedure was followed soldiers attempting to quell a riot might be charged with murder.

When the Hunt report on the police came out, it did indeed lead to the disarming of the R.U.C. and the disbandment of the 'B' Specials. Lord Hunt's main claim to fame was that he had climbed Mount Everest, but even so it might have occurred to him and the ministers he advised that if you demolish the existing police set-up, it is urgently necessary to put something effective in its place. With the 'B' Specials went the police intelligence, and the longer-term effect of the Hunt reforms was for the police more and more to leave their work to the army – including the detective work of the C.I.D.

Following on the very serious rioting in August 1969 and subsequent conferences at No. 10, Mr Wilson had considered installing a minister in Northern Ireland to keep an eye on Stormont. Lord Shackleton had been chosen for the job but on further consideration it had been thought his presence would undermine the authority of Mr Chichester-Clark and this idea was abandoned. Instead Mr Oliver Wright, until recently our Ambassador in Denmark, was installed at Stormont. Some difficulty was experienced owing to the fact that Northern Ireland was a Home Office responsibility while Mr Wright was in the Foreign Service. It is typical of the attitude of English people to Irish affairs that the appropriate channel of communication between Mr Wright and the government in London should have been seen as a problem, while a multitude of real, not merely procedural, problems were proliferating all around. Mr Wright, before he went to Denmark, had been in Mr Wilson's Cabinet Office. He had no wish to go to Northern Ireland and appears to have made little impact on the situation. His last words on leaving this appointment in March 1970 amounted to 'Cheer up, things are better than you think.' His successor was Ronald Burroughs, an expert on Portuguese affairs who had come to Mr Wilson's notice in connection with Rhodesian sanctions.

Events in the North and the inadequate protection given to the Catholics by the police led to the emergence of the I.R.A. into a new and active rôle. There is perhaps no need to go into the complicated manoeuvrings of the Dublin government – a weak and divided government presided over by Jack Lynch, a compromise Prime Minister. Ministers were under pressure to supply money or arms or both for the Northern Catholics but were embarrassed by the activities of British Intelligence Agents who often knew more of what was going on in the south than the Government itself. So it was to the I.R.A., not to the Dublin government, that the Catholics of the North eventually looked for protection. As we have seen, the I.R.A. was a body which had played an active part in Irish politics for many a long year. But more recently, under the leadership of Cathal Goulding it had moved to the Left and saw a solution of Irish problems in the setting up of a Marxist Republic. This led to growing tension between the Dublin leadership dreaming of a Communist Republic in the never-never land of the far future, and the Belfast leadership concerned with the here and now. The outcome was that in November 1969 Sean MacStiofain (who started out in life as John Stevenson) stamped out of a meeting in Dublin in which he had been outvoted by Goulding's men and announced the setting up of the Provisional Army Council with the declaration: 'We declare our allegiance to the 32 County Irish Republic proclaimed at Easter 1916, established by the first Dail in 1919, overthrown by force of arms in 1922 and suppressed to this day.'

In the early days the Provisionals, even in Belfast, seem to have been outnumbered by the Officials, and in any case the combined total was small. It was thought that the total number of activists in Belfast might have been eighty, of whom less than half were Provos. In the first months of 1970 the I.R.A. were more concerned with their internal problems than with longer-term objectives. Moreover, the position of the British Army vis-à-vis the Catholic population was not as antagonistic as it subsequently became. Also the necessary supplies of money and arms took time to organize.

In April there was serious rioting in Belfast and the extensive use of C.S. gas by the troops – an incident that provided an incentive for I.R.A. recruitment and a belief that the army was essentially hostile to Catholics. To our men on the spot – General Freeland and Ronald Burroughs – it was obvious from this episode that the traditional Orange Marches in the summer could only lead to serious trouble. However, Whitehall was pre-occupied with the General Election and the marches were in due course allowed to take place. It would be confusing to give the detailed history of a series of very similar disturbances. But the importance of the riots which took place between June and August was that they finally convinced the Catholics of Northern Ireland that the troops were their enemies and that protection could only come from the I.R.A. This impression was of course the result of no decision by the military authorities but was caused by an inadequate number of soldiers trying to keep order in an unfamiliar and very confused situation. Anyway, it was felt afterwards that it was in these months that any good feeling between the troops and the Catholics finally evaporated.

In subsequent months this feeling of antagonism was further enhanced by the behaviour of the troops, particularly in their searches of Catholic houses and their treatment of arrested men. It is not surprising under circumstances of great tension that prisoners received very rough treatment. Some of the arrested suspects were conspicuously innocent people whose names had been given by the I.R.A. specifically to bring the army into disrepute.

In the early summer the number of Provisional activists may have been 100, but by the end of the year it had risen to 800 and recruitment was going well.

During these months of 1970 when the situation in the Six Counties was going badly awry, there had been a change of government in London and the Minister responsible for Northern Ireland was now Mr Maudling instead of Mr Callaghan. The latter had done nothing effective, but had made a pleasing impression. Mr Maudling did nothing, but made a very unfavourable impression when he visited Belfast. He disliked the country, had not been shadow Home Secretary and so had not kept in touch with Irish affairs, of which he seemed wholly ignorant. He was supplied with a junior minister for Irish affairs, a Mr Sharples, who owed his promotion, it is said, to the fact that he had taught Mr Heath to sail.

Before the change of government it was credibly reported that Mr Callaghan had been planning to take over the government of Northern Ireland and a bill had been drafted with that intent. This was apparently not known to Mr Maudling when he took over. Mr Chichester-Clark, while proceeding with the agreed reforms, found himself under increasing pressure from his own back-benchers. To satisfy them he introduced draconian legislation for the maintenance of law and order and demanded military reinforcements. Relations between the troops and the Catholics deteriorated and in February 1971 the first soldier was killed. Administrative reforms, the reorganization of the police and the handing over of much of the law and order function to an inadequate military force did not add up to a policy which could conceivably bring peace to the Province.

Finally in March Chichester-Clark had had enough and decided to resign. He was one of the landed gentry who had ruled Northern Ireland for so long – his Chichester ancestors since the early sixteenth century. He was no politician, had tried to resign two months earlier but had been talked out of resignation at that time by Mr Heath.

His successor was Mr Brian Faulkner, a very different type. Welcomed by Mr Heath, who had known him when Mr Heath was President of the Board of Trade and Mr Faulkner was Minister of Commerce, he was seen as a 'professional', a welcome contrast to the amateurs who had preceded him. His record as Minister of Development under Mr Chichester-Clark had been quite good, a considerable contrast anyway from his period as a rabid Orangeman. He is not one of the landed gentry. His money comes from textiles and it is possible that his long wait for the top job – he had been twenty-two years a Stormont M.P. – was due to the fact that he was not on the same social level as the O'Neills and the Chichester-Clarks.

Mr Faulkner's first efforts at conciliation were to get members of the Opposition on to three important new committees – on social services, on the environment and on industrial development. They were to provide the chairman for two of them. Before this gesture could be implemented there was further serious rioting in Londonderry in which two men were killed. The soldiers who killed them were probably mistaken in taking the two for gunmen. Anyway, when an inquiry was refused, the Social Democrat and Labour Party walked out of Stormont and refused to have any more truck with Faulkner and the Stormont government.

A pet idea of Mr Faulkner's had been that internment without trial would have a valuable pacifying effect. Mr Faulkner had been Minister of Home Affairs in the previous period of I.R.A. activity between 1956 and 1962 and believed that internment at that time had had an important effect in defeating the campaign. Mr Chichester-Clark had been against internment as

147

they had insufficient information on the newer recruits to the I.R.A. and did not know whom to intern. However, when Mr Faulkner took over, internment was placed on the agenda. It was assumed that the internees would be Catholics. In the interval between Mr Faulkner's election in March and the introduction of internment in August there had been an average of two bomb explosions a day and four more soldiers were killed. The Army did not want internment but did not know what else to suggest. The British government thought the parallel between 1971 and 1959–62 was pretty shaky since in the earlier period there had been internment on both sides of the Border. However, Mr Faulkner seemed very confident, British ministers had nothing to suggest, so internment it was. It was thought at that time that there were perhaps 130 activist members of the I.R.A. of which 80 might be Provisionals. There were also some hundreds of sympathizers. The Army had had in mind the imprisonment of not more than 150, but Mr Faulkner, now he had got his internment, was determined on a clean sweep of 450 or more. In the outcome a very miscellaneous group of 342 were rounded up. The news of a probable decision on internment had leaked out and the Provisionals claimed, apparently justifiably, that their command structure had not been seriously affected.

It had been assumed by the Army that internment would cause a deterioration in the relations between the Catholics and the Army. It was also to be expected that there would be something of a backlash. It was hoped that both reactions would soon die down. The outcome was far worse than had been anticipated. In the four months before internment four soldiers and four civilians were killed. In the four months after internment the death-roll was 30 soldiers, 11 policemen and 73 civilians. 1576 had been arrested by the Army under the Special Powers Act – almost all Catholics – and it was no consolation that 934 were released shortly after their arrest. The impression left was that the original list of men to be 'lifted' was very carelessly drawn up. So many of the men were elderly that it was suspected that the list was one drawn up long ago.

The failure of internment was what shattered the British government's confidence in Mr Faulkner. He lingered on until March 1972, by which time his stock in Whitehall was very low indeed. He had made a gesture to the Opposition by appointing a Catholic to his Cabinet, but the Catholic he selected was not a man of influence in his community and the gesture was an empty one.

While the O'Neills, the Chichester-Clarks and the Faulkners were losing friends and failing to influence people, the principal figure to emerge on the Protestant side was Ian Paisley, Moderator of the Free Presbyterian Church. As a preacher he had an immense following in Northern Ireland, particularly in Belfast, where in 1969 he laid the foundation of a new church with seats for 2000 – and all of them needed. In 1970 he went into politics out of a sense of duty and won Bannside, O'Neill's old Stormont constituency. Later in the same year he won the Westminster seat of North Antrim, which includes Bannside. Though in religion he is a fundamentalist Protestant and in politics he had been a champion of the Protestant cause, he has been an excellent constituency M.P. with no bias against any section of the community. He is a big man and an honest man and a most gifted speaker able to deal in appropriate terms with an audience of M.P.s in Westminster or of shipyard workers in Belfast. It is because of his strong personality and his eloquence that he will continue to be a force to be reckoned with in Irish politics. Though he has received no recognition from the British government it is owing to his efforts that the Protestant reaction has not been far more violent, extending perhaps to civil war. The effect of the disturbances since 1969 has been to destroy the political power of the landed gentry and shift the centre of political gravity to the working classes who look to Paisley, to Craig of Vanguard, to Heron of the U.D.A. and to Hull of the Loyalists rather than to the old leadership of the Unionist Party.

On the Catholic side, we hear most of Mr Fitt, a Stormont and Westminster M.P., and of Mr Hume, Stormont M.P. for Londonderry, but it is the Provisional I.R.A. on whom the course of events principally depends. The dominant figure among the Provos was Sean MacStiofain, who was imprisoned in 1953 for stealing arms from a school at Felsted in Essex. He was at that time a railway shunter. His influence seems now on the wane and David O'Connell, a schoolteacher, is prominent in its counsels. Rory O'Brady, the political chief of the Provos, first came to prominence when he raided the Arborfield depot of the Royal Electrical and Mechanical Engineers and got away with five tons of arms. He was at that time a trainee teacher. Joe Cahill, a former docker, was at one time in command in Belfast; during the war he was nearly hanged for the murder of a policeman and he has lately been in the news for attempted gun-running in County Waterford.

In January 1972 I made a brief visit to Dublin and had talks with a variety of informants from Conor Cruise O'Brien on the Left to Dr Ryan, the newly nominated Archbishop of Dublin. I had talks with a number of newspaper people of various political complexions and was reliably briefed on the attitude of the I.R.A. leadership, and of the Dublin government. Needless to say, opinions covered a very wide range but there was unanimity on a few points: 1, that Stormont was finished; 2, that a military solution of the problems of Northern Ireland was not possible; 3, that the I.R.A. was not short of recruits and was confident of its ability to keep up its campaign indefinitely.

At the end of the month came Bloody Sunday in Londonderry, in which thirteen civilians were killed. This was followed by the burning of the British Embassy in Dublin. These events were by any standard unhelpful, but did not alter the essentials of the Irish problem. Mr Maudling continued to suggest a round table conference while the government set up an inquiry into the Londonderry shootings. The idea of a round table conference showed a complete lack of understanding of the situation at that point in time: the inquiry could only provide propaganda material favourable to the I.R.A. Round table conferences can only be expected to work where there is agreement on fundamentals, which is the last thing we have in Northern Ireland. Any solution will surely have to be an imposed one – and the only direction from which any initiative could come is from H.M.G.

Throughout these early months of 1972 it was increasingly assumed that Stormont had had its day. Mr Faulkner had got the British government to agree to internment as a set-off to the banning of Protestant marches but the result had been far worse than their worst fears. Confidence in Mr Faulkner's judgment sank to a low level in London where the impression gained ground that he did not keep British ministers fully in the picture. It was not until January that Paisley had an interview with the Prime Minister and it was only very gradually that ministers realized that Paisley is a man of real significance and not just a hooligan from the outback.

At the end of March the government suddenly announced that Stormont was being suspended and Northern Ireland was to come under direct rule from Westminster with William Whitelaw as Secretary of State. The move seems to have come as a surprise to Faulkner, and to have arisen over the question of security. Responsibility for the army and the police rested mainly on the government in London but also to an ill-defined degree on the government in Stormont. This was an unsatisfactory arrangement at best, but could only be made to work if there was complete confidence between Mr Heath and Mr Faulkner. This, unfortunately, had ceased to exist. The appointment of William Whitelaw was the best that could have been made. He was the outstanding member of the Heath Cabinet, a big man and one of immense charm. He knew nothing about Ireland and seems to have been under the impression that it would be possible to find an agreed solution. To the outsider it had seemed that the abolition of Stormont – albeit nominally for only one year – was the first step in a new departure by British policy. The removal of Stormont cleared the stage for the next act. Subsequent events showed that this was not the case. The decision was a limited one brought on by the continuing crisis in the security situation. The year was spent in looking for a painless solution to the problem of Northern Ireland ending with the White Paper, which is based on the assumption that an agreed solution is possible.

On taking over the Stormont administration ministers were aghast at the situation they found there. The degree of discrimination against the Catholics was far greater than had been expected, and the ranks of the civil service had been swollen by Unionist Party nominees. Deficiencies in the administration could only be corrected bit by bit, but a beginning was made with the release of internees in those cases where no valid reason appeared for their internment.

In a brief visit I made to Belfast at the end of April I met a wide variety of people. The near-unanimous opinion among Protestants was that Stormont in its old form was gone for good and what they wanted was complete integration with England. If this were not possible, a view I encountered was that notice should be served that the British government and army would be pulling out of Northern Ireland within a finite period of not more than ten years – perhaps only two. The argument was that if it were known the British were leaving, the attitude of the very realistic Protestants would change, while if they felt they would always be supported by British troops and British money there was no reason why they should not remain intransigent. In this connection there was some talk of an independent Northern Ireland. In the long run it would hardly

153

be viable but as a half-way house to a United Ireland it might have its points.

As his friends told him, the essential for Mr White-law was to keep the initiative, but after two months he had shaken a number of hands, impressed every-body with his fairness and charm, released a number of internees, but that was all. The trouble is that Ireland presents a purely political problem. It is not an administrative problem nor a financial one and only partly a military and security one, but neither Mr Whitelaw nor Mr Heath is a politician. The politi-cal atmosphere is clouded by the fact that leading members of the Government and of the Opposition maintain in private conversation that the only possible outcome is a United Ireland, while in public ministers keep on asserting that there will be no change without the consent of the majority which, obviously, will not be obtainable in the foreseeable future. The statements made in private leak out and build up a strong feeling of distrust in any undertaking by this government or any alternative British government.

By the end of June the Army in Northern Ireland had been reinforced but there was no sign of the political initiative which was already becoming over-due. The longer ministers were in charge of Irish affairs the more disenchanted they became with Mr Faulkner and the more disgusted with the former Stormont regime. But it was not clear that Mr Whitelaw's velvet glove contained a steel fist.

However, in July a truce was agreed by the I.R.A. It was a shaky affair, as the Dublin government, the I.R.A. and the Catholic hierarchy, let alone the British government and the Protestants, were apt to pursue their individual policies regardless of the other actors in the drama. Notwithstanding the difficulties, the truce could have provided a useful breathing space in which constructive policies could have been worked out. However, on July 9th the U.D.A. turned 200 Catholics out of their houses in Portadown. Whereupon the I.R.A. determined to put fifteen Catholic families into houses that had been allocated to them in the Lenadoon area of Belfast. The U.D.A. determined to resist this move. The army said that it would be impossible to move in the Catholic families that night without a major clash with the U.D.A. Mr Whitelaw was in Penrith and out of touch. In the outcome the army in effect took the side of the U.D.A. and the Catholics did not move in. The I.R.A. felt the army had intervened on the Protestant side in a dangerous situation and called off the truce. Whereupon one of Mr Whitelaw's officials put out a statement that the whole episode had been cooked up by the I.R.A. to provide an excuse for breaking off the truce. This was wildly untrue, as was afterwards admitted by Lord Carrington in the House of Lords. The I.R.A., feeling they had been unjustly aspersed, retaliated by stating that there had been a meeting of I.R.A. leaders and Mr Whitelaw in London a few days before. This was highly embarrassing to Mr Whitelaw. His reasons for meeting the I.R.A. himself were not obvious as he was in touch with them through other channels anyway. When this secret meeting was revealed Mr Whitelaw was furious, not with his officials for causing the revelation, but with the I.R.A. for their breach of confidence. Since that time he has not been in touch with the I.R.A. and has instead been readier to make optimistic statements about his determination to destroy the terrorists. The breakdown of the truce has diminished the authority of the more constructive I.R.A. leaders and reinforced the standing of the most militant. It is supposed that Mr Whitelaw met the I.R.A. leaders with a view to some kind of agreement. But this was never a possibility and, if it had been, should have been negotiated through third parties. The effect was necessarily to diminish Mr Whitelaw's influence both in Westminster and in Northern Ireland. The end of the truce was marked by greatly increased outbreaks of violence both in Belfast and in Londonderry. Another 4,000 troops were sent to Ireland and the whole outlook is worse than it has been for many years. However, one good thing was achieved with the additional troops; the no-go areas of Londonderry and Belfast were occupied by troops without bloodshed. The timing was bad – this should have been done after the abolition of Stormont, early in April, but better late than never. If the truce had been well handled it might have been possible to arrange for the dismantling of the barricades by agreement.

At the end of September Mr Whitelaw called a meeting of Northern Irish politicians, to take place at a hotel near Darlington. Many key figures refused to attend and there was no outcome of the meeting. It was difficult to see what results could have been expected.

At the end of October the government issued its Green Paper. It was well drafted, and favourably received by the politicians, though damned by the U.D.A. and the I.R.A. The paper is only issued as a basis for discussion but the implications are that security will remain with Westminster and that elections will be on the basis of Proportional Representation.

In early December I was in Dublin for a T.V. interview and took the opportunity of learning how opinion was moving in the I.R.A. camp. The British government had announced that they had dismissed with contempt an approach by the I.R.A. for a truce. Apparently there was no such approach. MacStiofain, the I.R.A. leader, had been dying while on hunger-strike, but was prevailed on by the Archbishop of Dublin and his predecessor to abandon it because of the bloodshed that would follow his death. Hunger-strike to the death was a conspicuous part of Republican tradition and Stevenson's abandonment of this tradition led to a great diminution of his influence. The Dublin government brought in an anti-terrorist bill that at one stage did not look like being passed. However, at the critical point in the debate a bomb went off near a cinema killing two and wounding more than a hundred. The obvious inference was that this was done by Protestants from the North in revenge for the bombings in Belfast. However, the timing was so exact for the maximum effect on the impending legislation that there were widespread suspicions in Dublin that the explosions were the work of the Irish – or perhaps the British – Secret Police. Anyway as a consequence of the explosion the legislation was duly passed.

Though Mr Whitelaw's prestige and influence were diminished by his unsuccessful bickering with the I.R.A. he was still generally liked and anyway regarded as much the most suitable British minister for the job.

He himself evidently found the job a severe strain – so much so that some of his friends thought he should be brought back to London.

Official statements were put out from time to time to say that at last the Army was getting on top of the terrorists. This was not true, but it was not clear whether these statements were actually believed by ministers, or were regarded as necessary propaganda to keep the party faithful to them.

The plebiscite on the Border was finally announced for March 8th. It had been promised nearly a year earlier but had been postponed for parliamentary reasons, and the White Paper, it was felt, could not be published until after the plebiscite. The plebiscite served no useful purpose – rather the reverse – but the long delay made it clear that when the government abolished Stormont they had no consequential moves in mind.

At the end of February, presumably to strengthen his hand in negotiations with the British government over the coming White Paper and legislation arising therefrom, Mr Lynch called a General Election. Apparently he was quite certain that he would win. But a hastily arranged coalition of Fine Gael and Labour concentrating on bread-and-butter issues won the election and Mr Lynch is out.

Towards the end of March the government at last published its White Paper on Northern Ireland. After such a long delay something more attractive might have been expected – and the Irish are great lovers of the dramatic. However, what it all boiled down to is: 1, no change in the status of Northern Ireland without majority consent; 2, the Army to remain in force indefinitely; 3, no increase in the number of Northern Ireland M.P.s at Westminster; 4, security to remain in the hands of Westminster; 5, administration of the Province to be in the hands of committees of the new Assembly in which all sections of the community would be represented, some committees – perhaps two – to be chaired by Catholics; 6, large powers to continue to be exercised by the Secretary of State for Northern Ireland; 7, a Council of Ireland to be set up – its function not clearly defined.

The proposals were immediately denounced by Dr Paisley and Mr Craig for the Protestants, and by the I.R.A. Faulkner for the Official Unionists accepted the proposals subject to modifications. Alliance and the Catholic S.D.L.P. were prepared to give the proposals a trial.

In the month following the issue of the White Paper attitudes thereto began to crystallize in the Six Counties. The opinion that emerged was that those prepared to work the White Paper and those determined to wreck it were represented about 50–50 in the Province, but that Faulkner and his Unionists would not be able to sustain their attitude and would have to demand substantial changes in the new constitution.

There have been rumours from time to time that Mr Whitelaw is on the point of return to London, where he has been tipped as the new Chancellor of the Exchequer. He has been at times in a nervous condition and has found Northern Ireland a traumatic experience, but those close to him believe he is determined to stay on, at least until the new Assembly is in good working order. The defeat of the I.R.A. by police and military means alone is not possible, and the

Assembly will not meet until July 31st, which would be a bit late in the career of this parliament for major ministerial changes. Ministers speak in private as if the success of the new Assembly is assured. They will learn – later.

The result of the elections at the end of June was to create, in effect, three substantial groups: 1, the Paisley–Craig anti-White Paper Protestants; 2, Faulkner and his more or less pro-White Paper Protestants; and 3, Gerry Fitt and the Catholic S.D.L.P. The Alliance Party, which is non-sectarian, did worse than it hoped and can have little influence on events. The significance of these results is the emergence of the Social Democrat and Labour Party as the accepted representative of the Catholics. Their nineteen seats in the new Stormont are a far higher proportion of the total than they had in the old Stormont. Though Gerry Fitt is the nominal leader of the party, Mr John Hume has emerged as the more effective personality. After all that has happened it is difficult to believe that Mr Faulkner will ever again be the leader of Northern Ireland. He is distrusted by too many people and is too closely associated with memories of the old Stormont. Prophecy about political events in Ireland is a very risky exercise, but it seems to me that Dr Paisley, with his many gifts, and advised by Desmond Boal, a very astute lawyer, is bound to emerge as the dominant figure in Ulster politics in the coming months. It is objected of him that he has said such ferocious things about Catholics in general, the Catholic Church and the Dublin government, that he cannot be the agent of Irish reconciliation. Personally, I am more optimistic. Politics in Ireland are often clothed in violent, indeed outrageous, language and this is well understood by all concerned. Furthermore Dr Paisley is a comparatively young man, in his middle forties, and he has shown a remarkable capacity for learning during his political career since 1970. Though to meet he is a forceful personality almost larger than life, it has to be borne in mind that he is deeply and sincerely religious, a man of prayer whose inner humility is much more important than his outward arrogance.

In Northern Ireland the proposal to keep law and order in the hands of the London government while keeping the Province's Westminster representation at twelve seemed indefensible. Surely they should have parliamentary representation pro rata to the rest of the United Kingdom, i.e. twenty or so M.P.s? The reason for this proviso was to secure bi-partisan support for the government's Irish policy in the House of Commons. Any increase in the number of Ulster M.P.s might go to the Conservatives and this would naturally be opposed by the Labour Party.

The proposal that the Province should be run by an administration that is 70 per cent Protestant and 30 per cent Catholic would seem unworkable in the conditions now prevailing. The violence and disorder continue unabated, though latterly the killing has been mainly between troops and I.R.A. and much less between local Catholics and Protestants as had been the case some months ago.

The White Paper did not seem a promising point of departure for people representing a wide range of opinion in the Six Counties. Would it not be better to give the Six Counties independence and let them work out their own relations with London and Dublin?

Many people feel that Irishmen would do better dealing with Irishmen without unhelpful meddling from London. Clearly independence for the Six Counties would need financial support from Great Britain, but such support should be less than it is at present, and most Englishmen would be glad to learn that Irish problems were no longer their responsibility and that our soldiers were no longer being killed and wounded.

Paisley, Craig and their friends want integration with Great Britain. If this is not to be had, and it isn't, they would prefer independence within the Commonwealth. British ministers have stated that independence would mean the withdrawal of financial support from London, and would lead to the wholesale massacre of Catholics. On the other hand the I.R.A., who are the people who would be massacred, do not think this would happen, nor does Dr Paisley and his group. If H.M.G. can part with the burden of Northern Ireland, why should they not be prepared to foot a reasonable part of the bill? The Republicans would see a great step forward in the departure of the British Army from Irish soil and the Protestants feel far more confident of coming to satisfactory terms with Dublin if there is no meddling from London.

CONCLUSION

In the belief that few Englishmen have any idea of Irish history I have set out in brief form the story of Anglo-Irish relations from very early times. The purpose is to show that the Irish are a very different people from the English and that this difference has been enhanced by the very different history of the two peoples.

The first point to be emphasized is that the indigenous Irish, though Celts, come from a different branch of that race than do the modern Welsh or the ancient Britons. Their culture was a rural one and there were no towns in Ireland, until those were founded by the Vikings many centuries after the foundation of the ancient cities of Great Britain. There were no roads until much later and there was no effective central government until comparatively modern times. The strong centralized administration of the Romans and the Normans was never established in Ireland.

When reading the history of Ireland before the twelfth-century invasion from England, the two main impressions of the Irish of that day are their great artistic talents together with their deep devotion to their religion. As all great art has a spiritual base, these two aspects of Irish culture may well be seen as two aspects of the same thing. These two qualities have remained

with the Irish down to the present day, though artistic-
ally they do not constitute the cultural centre of Europe
as they once did. The Book of Kells, the Cross of Cong
and the Ardagh Chalice show us what the Irish were
capable of. And was it not from Ireland that the
Church in north-eastern England was founded and
with its monasteries in Wearmouth, Lindisfarne and
Jarrow became in its day a centre of culture of European fame? When the Irish step on the stage of history
they are seen as artists and saints: their early monuments are religious, and abroad they are known for
their missionaries, of whom St Patrick was only one of
those celebrated in their day.

One does not need to be starry-eyed about the
early Irish. Tribal warfare was endemic: cattle raids
were a permanent feature of their society. They were
not traders on any scale. This, too, has persisted to the
present day. Though three of the richest American
families, Ford, Mellon and Kennedy, are all Irish,
money-making is not a dominant trait in the Irish
character. They are a very sociable people – good
talk is more highly valued in Ireland than elsewhere;
hence in part their appreciation of alcoholic drink
– it helps make a party go, and in later centuries
gave a brief respite from despair.

As Dr Paisley once said to me, Ireland's troubles
were begun by the Pope. I asked why, and he said it
was the Pope who granted Ireland to Henry II.
Whether or not this grant made much difference, it
was the invasion of Ireland by Strongbow that began
the relationship which has continued for 800 years its
tragic course between Ireland and Great Britain. The
great chronicler Giraldus Cambrensis, writing at the

beginning of the thirteenth century, made a remarkably prophetic statement:

> The Irish had not so strictly offended God that it was His will that they should be entirely subjugated: nor were the deserts of the English such as to entitle them to the Sovereignty over and possible obedience of the people they had partly conquered and reduced to obedience. Therefore, perhaps, it was the will of God that both nations would be long engaged in mutual conflicts. (*The Lordship of Ireland in the Middle Ages.*)

The Normans with their more advanced weapons and methods of warfare defeated the Irish but failed to establish a firm grip over the whole country. There were no roads and no centres of population away from the coast and, unlike the present day, the country was thickly wooded. A centre of administration and English authority was set up in Dublin but there was no continuous English jurisdiction over the rest of the country. In the course of succeeding centuries the Norman English families gradually became absorbed into Irish society until the distinction between the native Irish and the old English became a narrow one. However, even in those distant times the English from England had developed a contempt for what are called in ancient documents the 'wild Irish'. Crimes by the English against the Irish were regarded in the same light as crimes against the aborigines in the last century by Australian settlers. Killing a native was seen as a trivial event comparable with the destruction of some noxious animal. This contempt is of course a necessary morale booster for people who find themselves in an exposed situation under threat from a more numerous indigenous population. Three thousand Englishmen could not have ruled two hundred million Indians without a sense of conscious superiority, however ill-founded that may have been. So treating the native Irish as contemptible creatures outside the law was necessary for the morale of the English minority and contributed an element of terror to keep the wild Irish in place. However, by the beginning of the sixteenth century the Pale round Dublin had shrunk to small dimensions and the 'old English' were far more Irish than English – in many cases even Irish-speaking.

The sixteenth century saw a complete change in the situation owing to the threat to English sovereignty from the great continental powers France and Spain. The English attitudes to Ireland have at different times reflected fear, greed or exasperation. In Tudor and Stuart times the dominant attitude was fear. Threatened by the far more powerful countries of the Continent it was essential that they should be prevented from setting up a military base in Ireland, thus taking England in the rear. Hence the military campaigns against the Irish in the reign of Elizabeth, and the plantations under the Stuarts, and the final subjugation of the Irish by Cromwell. The defeat of James II at the Battle of the Boyne confirmed the earlier operations. The planting of settlers in the south of Ireland was a failure but did lead to the ownership of almost all Irish real estate passing to English landlords. The planting in Ulster of English, but mostly Scottish, settlers was a success and leads us to the troubles in Northern Ireland today. The idea was to have a resident garrison of reliable colonists in what had been the most rebellious part of all Ireland. They were a different people from their southern neighbours, their farmers had rights vis-à-vis their landlords as the southern Irish had not, and it was they who developed the textile and subsequently the ship-building industries of Ulster and made Belfast the only industrial city in the whole of Ireland.

In the eighteenth century fear of the Continental powers subsided and the two dominating factors were a rapidly rising population and the greed of mostly English landlords to squeeze the last farthing out of their tenants by any means at their disposal. The agitation for some measure of self-government which made some progress from the last quarter of the eighteenth century was Protestant-led and was mainly a protest against the appalling misgovernment of the country by the authorities in London. Up to this point political agitation in Ireland had not been sectarian. The Rebellion of 1798 had two centres, one in Presbyterian Ulster and the other in Catholic Wexford. But with the new century the Presbyterians and Anglicans of Ulster saw that their commercial prosperity depended on the union with England and remained firmly attached to the British connection.

The misery of the Irish peasant reached its climax in the Famine of the years from 1846. This terrible tragedy is one cause of the incomprehension subsisting between the English and the Irish. The most catastrophic event in the domestic history of these islands since the Black Death of the fourteenth century is just a non-event to the ordinary Englishman, whereas to the Irishman it is the supreme example of the callous

167

misgovernment of Ireland by ignorant Englishmen in London. It has led and still leads to bitter hostility to England from men of Irish descent anywhere in the world. But even the Woods and the Trevelyans were not wholly unmoved by the halving of the Irish population by starvation and emigration, and from then on British opinion has been to some extent motivated by a guilty conscience. A guilty conscience is no bad thing, but on the Irish side they, too, had learnt a lesson taught them by the achievement of Catholic emancipation in 1829 followed by the great Reform Bill of 1832. British governments, they learned, do not yield to persuasion – only to violence or the threat thereof. If the Liberals had made the same observation in England and laid in a stock of hand grenades we should have had Proportional Representation years and years ago.

It was by terrorist tactics that successive British governments were pushed into buying out Irish landlords and making Ireland a country of peasant proprietors. It was owing to continued violence that Home Rule was kept in the forefront of British politics from 1886, and it was through the violence of 1916 and the subsequent 'troubles' that southern Ireland secured its independence in 1922. Throughout Anglo-Irish history the story is one of half-hearted coercion followed by half-hearted conciliation – both policies being pursued by Englishmen in London ignorant of Ireland, of the Irish and of Irish history. If you want to see British governmental incompetence at its worst, study Whitehall from a stance in Ireland. The English were powerful enough, though not ruthless enough, to turn Ireland into a colony of helots. They were rich enough, though not wise enough, to turn Ireland into the friendliest of neighbours. So the Irish problem has bedevilled England off and on for eight hundred years and the end is not yet.

The settlement of 1922 gave the nationalists of southern Ireland the essentials of what they wanted. Being a contrary people, they waged a bitter civil war over the fine print of the agreement and let the partition of Ireland go almost by default. The Unionists of Ulster by the threat of force intimidated the British Government into giving them the Six Counties – the classic case of gerrymandering in these islands. At that time no one thought the settlement would be a lasting one but something had to be done to stop the killing and this was the best that could be managed at the time. The Protestants of the north, a practical people, used their semi-independence to make their control of the Six Counties positively ironclad; those of the 26 counties, an emotional and imaginative people, squabbled and fought over the exact status of the Crown – a squabble which has its repercussions down to the present day. The British government, glad to get Ireland out of its hair, hardly gave its neighbouring island a thought except when demands of Irish Nationalists for a greater degree of legal independence were met in the late 'thirties and ten years later. Though politically a sovereign state, in matters of currency, trade and employment it is a dependency of England – now as before.

It is significant that when trouble broke out in Northern Ireland in 1969, British ministers, instead of seeing in these events a return to the 'troubles', seem to have treated the business as if it were comparable with the farcical Anguilla episode. And it is

169

not clear that Mr Heath's administration is much more realistic. A kind word here and there and a few administrative reforms were supposedly all that was required from Mr Callaghan, and now Mr White- law's abundant charm is expected to turn the trick. But the Irish know all about charm and though they like Mr Whitelaw it will need more than words and smiles to restore peace to Ireland. It would help if Mr Whitelaw could refrain from promises to root out the terrorists. How does one root out Irish history? Mr Heath, too, might refrain from urging the people of Northern Ireland to raise their standard of behaviour to that prevailing in Margate.

It would be helpful if what people say in private were also said in public. Politicians in Westminster who have been closest to recent events in Ireland are con- vinced that the only answer is a United Ireland. The problems are how and when. It is common ground that there is no military solution to the problems of Northern Ireland and that the army cannot be kept there indefinitely on police duty without becoming demoralized. And of this there have been signs. It is unrealistic to expect a body of young men recruited and trained for a quite different purpose to stand up to urban guerrilla warfare in support of a non-existent British policy, without their patience and control giv- ing way from time to time.

The I.R.A. are well aware that it was they who destroyed Stormont and they regard themselves with some plausibility as the successors of the Irish freedom fighters from 1798 to modern times. It would seem to me that once Stormont in its old form had gone there was more to be got by diplomatic means than by continuing violence. However, that is not how it seems to them.

While the British Army and British finance are committed to the Six Counties, the Protestants will concede nothing. Why should they? Thanks largely to Dr Paisley, at critical moments they have shown much patience in the face of great provocation. But the Protestant private armies are more numerous, better armed and drilled than their Catholic counterparts. The knowledge that these forces exist has prevented the British government coming out with any policy of its own. It declines to take any constructive initiative, hoping that an agreed solution will be reached by the new Assembly. My own impression is that the Protestant Ulsterman is above all practical and when he realizes that things have changed and that the Six Counties are no longer the cherished darlings of the British government, he will use his great powers of leverage to do the best possible deal – financial with London, political with Dublin.

And the British government might consider a few elementary political points. There are two answers to terrorism – conciliation or counter-terror. The latter would involve the deaths of many hundreds, perhaps thousands, of men and women without trial. Such a policy in the hands of the S.S. would work for a generation, perhaps longer, but is not available to a British government. So they are left with conciliation. They might also consider that there is only one possible punishment for treason and that is death. Imprisonment when dealing with militant nationalists is an accolade, not a punishment. Nehru, Gandhi, Nkrumah, de Valera, Makarios, Kenyatta and many others built their careers on sentences of imprisonment. The prisons in Northern Ireland have become training grounds for the I.R.A. cadres of the future. By charging men who wage war against Her Majesty the Queen (the definition of treason) with civilian offences and then abolishing capital punishment for murder, the government of Northern Ireland is depriving themselves of the only deterrent. At one time all the I.R.A. wanted was a declaration that the future of Ireland was a matter for the Irish. Is there not wisdom in this? For all his talk of his attachment to the British way of life, the Ulsterman is far more Irish than English, and in matters of religion and sport Ireland is already united.

I will conclude with a quotation from a letter written by the great Duke of Wellington to his brother, Marquess Wellesley, in 1812. He said that it was only religious divisions which kept Ireland for the Empire, by turning the Protestants into a privileged garrison, afraid of the Catholics, 'Abolish the distinction, and make all Irishmen alike and they will all have Irish feelings, which tend towards independence and separation.'

INDEX